earth
&soul

earth & soul

RECONNECTING AMID CLIMATE CHAOS

LEAH RAMPY

BOLD STORY PRESS

CHEVY CHASE, MARYLAND

Bold Story Press, Chevy Chase, MD 20815
www.boldstorypress.com

Acknowledgements for Permission to Reprint

1. Quote in Chapter 3 (p. 52) from Stephen Harrod Buhner, *Earth Grief; The Journey into and through Ecological Loss*. (Boulder, CO: Raven Press, 2022), 256. Reprinted by permission of the Trustee, Stephen Harrod Buhner Trust.

2. Quote in Chapter 4 (p. 55) from Maria Popova, "Barry Lopez on the Cure for Our Existential Loneliness and the Three Tenets of a Full Life," *The Marginalian* (blog), September 18, 2022, https://www.themarginalian.org/2022/09/18/barry-lopez-place-loneliness/. Reprinted by permission of the author.

3. An earlier version of Chapter 5, Coming to Our Senses, first appeared as Chapter 10, "Coming to Our Senses: Embracing Wonder and Gratitude" by Leah Moran Rampy from Westina Matthews, Margaret Benefiel, Jackson Droney, editors. *Soul Food: Nourishing Essays on Contemplative Living and Leadership*. (New York: Church Publishing, 2023) 119–130. Reprinted by permission of the publisher.

4. Quote in Chapter 6 (p. 94) from Trebbe Johnson, *Radical Joy for Hard Times: Finding Meaning and Making Beauty in Earth's Broken Places* (Berkeley, CA: North Atlantic Books, 2018) 206. Reprinted by permission of the publisher.

5. Quote in Chapter 7 (p. 105) from Sharon Blackie, *If Women Rose Rooted; The Journey to Authenticity and Belonging* (London, United Kingdom: September Publishing, 2016), 132–33. Reprinted by permission of the publisher.

First edition: February 2024

Library of Congress Control Number: 2023917638

ISBN: 978-1-954805-62-0 (paperback)
ISBN: 978-1-954805-63-7 (e-book)

Text and cover design by KP Design
Author photo by Leslie Williams

Printed in the United States of America
10   9   8   7   6   5   4   3   2   1

In memory of Mom and Dad

With love to David, Andrew, and Ana

Table of Contents

Introduction

*We have forgotten who we are and have fallen
out of true relationship with the earth and
with one another. Thus, the path to well-being
is not about becoming something other than
ourselves. . . . It is about waking up to a knowledge
that is deep in the very fabric of our being. . . .*[1]

JOHN PHILIP NEWELL

A legend among some Native American tribes is told by elders in times of great difficulty.[2] It is of an old woman, deep in a cave, weaving the world. Light and shadows dance around her as she weaves. She has been weaving a long lifetime, and the garment born of her dreams and dedication is of exquisite beauty. The only time she leaves her loom is to go far back into the cave to stir the contents of a pot simmering over the oldest fire in the world. It contains the roots and seeds of all the plants, herbs, and grains that feed the Earth. If she does not stir this elemental soup, it may burn, and who knows what trouble that may cause.

Living in the cave with her is a black dog who dozes while the woman works at her loom. When she rises to tend the pot, the dog rouses. While she shuffles slowly—after all she is very old—to the back of the cave, the dog grabs a loose thread in his teeth and begins to pull. As the old woman painstakingly makes her way to and from the fire, the dog tugs at various threads, pulling until finally the weaving comes apart and the threads are scattered across the cave floor.

Upon her return, the old woman sees the product of her long labor in disarray, her efforts turned to naught. She gazes upon what remains, sitting silently for some time. Slowly she bends to pick up a thread. Soon the original pattern is forgotten as a new and previously unimagined design of great beauty takes shape in her mind's eye. Guided by this vision, her old hands begin to weave a beautiful tapestry from the chaos.

I heard this story in three different venues before it tucked itself into my thoughts, and I began to ponder more deeply its message. What wisdom do such ancient stories offer us about living in these chaotic times?

▪ ▪ ▪

I awake in the darkness to NPR news: Fort Lauderdale has received 25 inches of rain in seven hours. The land is inundated. The previous record rainfall was 17 inches *in the entire month*. Such news should be shocking, but this decade of weather chaos has left us more resigned than surprised. Terms we never knew have slipped into the vernacular: *polar vortex*, *firenado*, *bomb cyclone, atmospheric river, thundersnow, flash drought,* and *derecho.*[3]

Like many others, our family experienced a derecho before we knew such a weather feature existed. It had been an unremarkable summer day on June 29, 2012, although 104°F was unusually hot for this time of year in the Washington, DC metro area. Our teenage son sat on the porch talking with a friend as they noted the coming thunderstorm. When the powerful, straight-line storm struck, the combination of furious winds, driving rain, and ground lightning ripped around us—and sent even mortality-denying teenagers indoors. We huddled away from windows, certain that any moment an uprooted tree would make an uninvited appearance.

After pounding on windows and doors for nearly an hour, the winds took their leave, and we were able to assess the damage. In addition to a swath of branches and leaves around the yard, a tree had split in half and was lying across the road. Tragically, thirteen people had been killed, and millions of people from Ohio to DC were left without power. The ensuing heat wave would claim another thirty-four lives.[4]

Meteorologists commented on the never-before-seen number of lightning strikes accompanied by rain and intense winds—over 70 mph measured at Dulles International Airport; these were a portent of what was to come.[5] The climate was becoming increasingly unstable.

Fast forward nine years to the day in the tiny town of Forks, Washington, on the opposite coast. Made famous by the Twilight novels of Stephenie Meyer, Forks offers tourists a vampire/werewolf vibe as well as proximity to rainforest and beaches. The town boasts an "enjoyable" average high temperature in June of 61.3°F. However, on

June 29, 2021, Forks set a record high of 108°F—nearly forty-seven degrees above average.[6] Forks townsfolk did not suffer alone. Nearly one in three Americans experienced a weather disaster in the summer of 2021: floods, hurricanes, storms, wildfires, chronic drought.[7] Nearly two-thirds of the population faced life-threatening, multi-day heat waves.[8]

The derecho of 2012 was considered one of the worst storms in DC history. Then the most intense rainstorm to hit the capital region arrived on the scene in August 2023, with winds up to 84 mph. The temperatures in Forks seemed outrageous until Phoenix suffered through thirty-four straight days of over 110 degrees in mid-summer of 2023, the temperature at 4,000 feet in the Andes topped 95 degrees during July the same year (winter in the Southern Hemisphere), and over and over new records were set for the hottest day on Earth in 125,000 years. Waters off the coast of Florida exceeded 100 degrees, and ocean temperatures jumped to new highs. Climate scientists predict that 2023 will be the hottest year in current history, and 2024 may be hotter still. [9]

We have changed Earth forever. This is not a book about climate chaos or ecosystem loss, but I will explore these issues briefly over the next few pages to set the stage for deeper conversations, for this is the environment in which we are living. We cannot return to times gone by; to know the loss and to allow our hearts to be broken by that knowledge is critical to the work to which we are called. Only when broken open will our hearts be large enough to hold the beauty and wonder as we face sorrow and grief. Only when we look clearly at what is happening will we build the fortitude and resolve necessary to reconnect with Earth and work toward the dream she is weaving anew.

■ ■ ■

My climate journey began in earnest in 2013 when our teenage daughter and I traveled to Chicago for Climate Reality training. Al Gore delivered his updated slideshow introduced in the movie *An Inconvenient Truth.* Then, the former vice president of the United States carefully broke down the details, shared the research, and illustrated the results of decades of burning fossil fuels. We came away sobered, concerned, and committed to spreading the word about what was happening to this world.

One clear goal we shared with other newly minted climate leaders: keep the parts per million (ppm) of carbon dioxide (CO_2) from exceeding 400. But despite the efforts of thousands of energetic and well-trained climate ambassadors and nonprofit leaders working around the globe, results for 2020 showed a record high of 412.5 ppm, even with reduced emissions resulting from the pandemic. This level is higher than any point in the last 800,000 years.[10]

Ancient air bubbles trapped in mile-thick ice cores show that CO_2 and temperature have risen and fallen in a synchronous pattern. When carbon dioxide is out of balance, it traps additional heat in the atmosphere and drives up the Earth's temperature. Earth's hottest month on record thus far: July 2023.[11]

Meanwhile the entire world feels the effects of the unrestrained burning of fossil fuels. With every increased degree Celsius, the air holds seven percent more moisture, which results in more intense rainfall.[12] From Germany to Sudan, over 700,000 people experienced the devastation of extensive flooding in the summer of 2021. In both China and New York, people were trapped in subways and basements by fast-rising waters.

Floods do little to address the effects of drought. Fast and furious rainfall cannot soak into the ground to be stored in underground springs and rivers; instead, torrents of water run quickly off the land, carving new pathways, too often taking property and lives, and carrying precious topsoil to the sea. Add higher temperatures to drought conditions, and you get fire seasons that start earlier and last longer, and fires that burn hotter.

In early August 2021, the secretary-general of the United Nations, António Guterres, declared a "Code Red for humanity" based on what he termed irrefutable evidence that the planet has warmed nearly 2°F since the beginning of the industrial revolution.[13] The National Oceanic and Atmospheric Administration's *State of the Climate in 2020* report cited record-high levels of greenhouse gas, "unprecedented" global sea levels, and "unprecedented warmth."[14] We could add unprecedented melting of glaciers and permafrost to this bleak picture. Earth is on fire, and we are fanning the flames.

The impact of climate chaos is not limited to humans. Species and ecosystems have been taking a huge hit. Forty-seven percent of species already have lost some of their populations due to climate change, and one million plant and animal species are at risk of extinction within years, not decades. Two-thirds of the wildlife has vanished since 1970; it will take five to seven million years to recover what was lost in the past fifty years.[15] At the current rate, death is proceeding more rapidly than new plants and animals can evolve to take the place of those that have been lost. Every twenty minutes, a plant or animal species becomes extinct, a pace 100 to 1,000 times faster than the background rate found in fossil records.[16]

The loss of the ecosystems that serve as habitat for plants and animals is even more dramatic. Only three percent of the world's land ecosystems remain intact; only 11 percent can support the species that once lived there.[17] More than 1,400 tree species are assessed as critically endangered[18]

The beautiful, exquisitely woven fabric of Earth is being unraveled. There is no reset button on life that has been extinguished; there is no reinstallation of the original operating system for ecosystems already destroyed.

I had hoped to make a difference by educating people about climate change. Slowly, it dawned on me that the lens I was using was too small for the scope of the challenges we face. Human actions that lead to climate change and biodiversity loss are based on a series of assumptions about our relationship—or lack thereof—to the living world. Too many of us too often have treated *nature* as inert resources available primarily for the benefit of humans. We have been clawing at the tapestry of the Earth, pulling at the threads that connect us so that we might serve our immediate wants and needs. We have suppressed the wisdom of our souls and frayed our ties to the fabric of the cosmos. Soul and Earth cry out for a conversation far deeper and more profound than that of saving our lifestyle. It is time to reweave connections for the sake of mutual thriving, here and now, as we teeter on the edge of even greater climate chaos and loss.

■ ■ ■

It's said that the ancient Celts of Ireland and Scotland used to travel to the edges of their home islands to seek wisdom and deeper connection. Edges—where sea, land, and sky meet—were considered sacred, *thin* places. When you stand at an edge, the division between heaven and earth, past and present, living and dead can blur, and a sense of oneness permeates time and place. In my work leading contemplative pilgrimages, I've been honored to travel to many places. Six times I've taken groups to the Scottish isle of Iona, where pilgrims have sought refuge and inspiration for several thousand years, soaking the earth with their prayers in this thin place where edges invite a sense of deep connection to the sacred.

Biologists and others who know the land tell us that *edges* are special for another reason. Where one ecosystem meets another—land meets sea, forest melds into fields, marsh runs to river—there arises an in-between place called an *ecotone*. An ecotone hosts a unique and hospitable environment where diverse flora and fauna can flourish on the edge of other systems. However, if human interference infringes on an ecotone, biodiversity diminishes, and ecotones become harsh and dangerous places.

Surely this example has much to teach us metaphorically and literally about mutual thriving in edge times. We are called to hear and respond to Earth's cry, to understand our niche in supporting life. As members of the Earth family, we, too, have been bestowed with gifts that are needed during these times of unraveling and creating anew. We are here to live into our unique calling in this in-between time on the edge of increasing losses.

I am not the first to suggest that the crisis we face today is a spiritual one. Without attending to our own continued transformation, we cannot hope to align with the living world to create a tapestry of a beautiful future. Indeed, if we do not cultivate heart and soul, we may not even *recognize* our increasing disconnection to our cosmic home. As we embrace more fully the sacred mystery within, around, and beyond ourselves, we may sense a wordless communion. In this contemplative experience, we remember that we are one.

Contemplative experiences of heart and soul are difficult to articulate. As a retreat leader, I've noticed that the deeper an experience is for participants, the more they struggle to describe it. Their voice is often halting, the words come slowly, there is a drawing inward as the person searches for words that might illuminate their experience. Sometimes we are simply not ready for words; sometimes the experience will be beyond words.

Through the ages, mystics and sages have tried to define *contemplation*. Jesuit theologian Walter Burghardt described it as a "long, loving look at the real."[19] This description recalls a comment I once heard author Scott Russel Sanders make about times when "... we disappear into the seeing." Without judgment, names, or labels, our senses perceive oneness with the sacred in everything. For many of us, the natural world is a doorway to deep mystery, unity, and communion. As we journey together, we'll explore practices to support our availability for deep connection. Of course, contemplation may come unexpectedly and be seemingly independent of any practice we might have engaged; then all that is required of us is to receive this holy gift.

■ ■ ■

My understanding of the Cosmic Sacred in whom we live and move and have our being is always evolving. You may have noticed that I have no clear name to encompass that holy mystery. Some might use the name *God*. Because that name is attached to limiting stories from my childhood, it evokes a presence too small for the vastness of the sacred as I understand it today. I include terms like *wisdom*, *holy*, *sacred*, *mystery*, and others as I seek to expand my thinking. I am interested in the deep, universal power of loving communion—and all words are woefully inadequate to express that. I hope that my use of multiple terms will free you to substitute the words most aligned with your own understanding—from your tradition or no tradition—or perhaps even free to you to explore the edges of your understanding.

Another term that bears examination in our work together is *soul*. Perhaps you were taught that body and soul are separate and distinct entities or even that your body might lead you astray, while your soul would gain you access to a higher realm. This is not how I will use the term.

I'm indebted to the Celtic understanding that does not limit soul in time or space. All aspects of you are contained within the light of the soul that encompasses and exceeds your body. One's soul reveals one's unique gifts to the world—and simultaneously is woven into the universal web. I do not assume that soul is a uniquely human characteristic; all beings live in soul communion with each other. We cannot be torn apart, but we can, and often do, forget our unity and fray the threads of connection.

◼ ◼ ◼

On the isle of Iona as well as other Hebridean islands, you'll find a unique ecotone called a *machair* (`makər). It is a low-lying field formed when sand and bits of shell from the adjacent coastline are blown by strong ocean winds beyond the sand dunes onto the land. Add just the right amount of rainfall and grazing animals and you get an abundant pasture of plants and wildflowers. The flowers attract invertebrates, which in turn draw birds to the machair to feed and breed. The "crex-crex" of elusive and nearly extinct corncrakes can sometimes be heard from their hiding places on the machair as they take a break on their long journey to their winter home in Africa.

On Iona, the machair serves as a community pasture for sheep, an open-to-all golf course, and the pilgrim's route to St. Columba's beach. As you walk the machair to the bay, each footstep is cradled by tiny wildflowers of buttercup yellow and daisy white. This thin place of wild sea, sky, and earth is harsh, rugged, beautiful and fragile, susceptible to climate change, sea level rise, and increasing storms. It is one example of an ecotone on the edge.

In this time on the edge, all of us, like the birds of the machair, are thrust into emerging ecotones that we have yet to fully understand, plunged into a changing environment unlike anything we have known. There is no going back— for humans, plants, birds, insects, or mammals—as much of the life we once knew has been or is being destroyed.

We have arrived at the edge. We have arrived, often before fully recognizing our soul purpose and without the internal resources we will need for this chaotic time of unraveling the past and envisioning the future. Through no fault of our own, some of us will find ourselves in the path of destruction. Others will refuse to accept change and will cling too long to a disappearing past. Yet perhaps it's not too much to hope that some of us will answer our soul's calling and seek the transformation necessary to participate in a new vision for the well-being of all.

Over the last decade, I have co-led contemplative pilgrimages to Iona, the Olympic Peninsula, Newfoundland,

and Cuba because I am convinced that traveling with a pilgrim heart has much to teach us. In this book, you're invited on a pilgrimage like no other. To begin our quest, we will need to summon courage for a long, loving look at the real so that we might discover beauty in the broken and possibility in the grief. Our mission is to embrace a growing love for and communion within the web of life and to enter the story of mutual thriving. Regardless of our age, our hope is to act as wise elders to future generations, laying steppingstones to a world of oneness, vibrancy, and liveliness beyond the limits of our lifetime. Here, in these edge times, we may join in reweaving the beautiful, life-giving tapestry of Earth and soul.

ONE

Connections

■

It really boils down to this: that all life is interrelated.
We are all caught in an inescapable network of
mutuality, tied into a single garment of destiny.
Whatever affects one directly, affects all indirectly.[1]

MARTIN LUTHER KING, JR.

Ripening wheat extends in every direction, tall, golden-yellow stalks contrasting with the muted green yard of wiry buffalo grass around our house. There's always wind in Kansas, but today the breeze is only strong enough to chase the billowy clouds from the sky and flutter the sheets on the clothesline. The outstretched arms of cedars brush against me, prompting memories of warm hats and woolen sweaters freed each November from their summer confinement in Mother's cedar chest. Pulling the skirt of my print dress snugly beneath me, I sit cross-legged on the walkway between the trees and reach out to stroke the leaves of these green giants. I am five years old.

Sunlight streams through cedar branches, dancing and dazzling. The brilliant blue berries are tiny, marble round, and perfectly sized for my small hands; the leaves of interlocking scales, smooth; the reddish-brown fibrous strips of bark, ready for squirrel nests and weavings. Diligently I plop the berries into my bright yellow sand bucket.

I much prefer my version of berry picking to afternoons with my mother gathering wild currants along weed-choked roadsides. I like hearing the conversations between my mother and her friend Daisy, but filling the buckets with ripe berries is always accompanied by itchy red chigger bites that keep me scratching all night around circles of pink calamine.

I knew my cedars well and could easily recognize their relatives on rocky limestone outcroppings from the back seat of the family Chevy, where I sat with my nose pressed against the window. Mom and Dad paid little attention to them as we made our way to church or to town for groceries. To me, they felt like part of my family.

■ ■ ■

Noted on the website of a Kansas arboretum: "Trees grow easily, but not here. A good shade tree in Kansas is a luxury."[2] Months of drought followed by intense bursts of rain, sweltering heat in summer, below-zero temperatures in winter, blizzards raging across the open prairie—most trees do not find this a happy place. However, the dearth of trees was not for a lack of trying on the part of the government and early settlers.

Wild and empty space as far as the eye could see presented an unfamiliar landscape to the early European homesteaders resettling in the High Plains. They followed the same pattern practiced by immigrants in other parts of the country: Do your best to tame and reform the landscape in the image of the homeland. Kansans were supported in this effort by President Theodore Roosevelt who oversaw the dedication of 97,280 acres to create the Garden City (Kansas) National Forest in 1906 and subsequently more than tripled the size of the original grant to create the Kansas National Forest in 1908.

There's a reason you've never heard of this Kansas forest: It was abolished in 1915. Prairie fires and drought killed most of the 800,000 seedlings planted there. Records note that, at the end of this nine-year experiment, the strongest trees remaining were a few yellow pines about two feet tall.[3]

Drive the highways and byways of central and western Kansas and you will become acquainted with the gently rolling and mostly treeless landscape. Chances are, the few trees you will see will be eastern red cedars growing on bluffs or occasionally in pastures, and cottonwoods gathered along a dry creek bed. While my contemporaries in other parts of the country were getting to know a variety of tree species, my childhood was bounded by the native cedars and cottonwoods.

The eastern red cedar is not a true cedar but an evergreen juniper. These trees would likely have spread across the open land before settlers arrived, but fire management by Native tribes limited them to rocky outcroppings, bluffs, or draws, where they could survive the blazes. When settlers arrived and the people who had cared for the land were pushed farther west, fire management ceased. Then began the ripping open of this rich grassland ecosystem to create farmland. Without the deep roots of the native grasses to hold the soil in place, it took only a few routine droughts to create the Dust Bowl of the 1930s. During this time the farmers lost an unfathomable 480 tons of topsoil *per acre.*

"Shelter belts" were one of the remedies designed to tame the relentless blowing dirt of the Dirty Thirties. Lengths of trees were planted along fence rows on every square-mile section to serve as wind breaks. Because they thrived in the harshness of Kansas weather, cedars were often selected for this role. These rows of cedars served as refuge for pheasants, quail, songbirds, turkey, bobwhites, and ruffled grouse, as well as cover for insects and small mammals.[4] The downside: Without the managed burns, abundantly thriving cedars crowded out other trees that offered diverse gifts.

Long before I sat in the Kansas dirt picking cedar berries, Native American cultures acknowledged the importance of the eastern red cedar, calling it "the Tree of Life."[5] It takes three years under ideal conditions for the berries of the cedar to change from flowers to green berries to blue; that's when they become gifts of food and medicine. The berries offer the human palate a mild, slightly woody taste, but without the slight bitterness of common juniper berries. Cedar berries are food to more than fifty bird species[6] and were used for shelters, boat making, and basket making. Though appearing scrubby and unimpressive to the uninformed, eastern red cedars offer gifts aplenty to those who know how to connect with them.

Although it's only the cedars that live in my memory, old black-and-white photos from my early childhood show a grove of more than thirty small trees planted along the north side of our yard, their images now too indistinct to make identification possible. All these trees are gone now, as are the house, garden, outbuildings, and anyone who might remember this place I knew so well as a child. Only the access leading from the main gravel road to our dirt road remains, an echo of another lifetime. Fields of wheat and oil wells have claimed it all.

The trees are gone. Imagine the possibilities if they had been left to grow. What beautiful gifts they might have become: sequestering carbon, purifying the air, creating soil, birthing new trees, drawing rainwater into the massive underground Ogallala aquifer, offering welcome shade in which farmers could pause for lunch. Families might come for picnics or walks among those graceful old beauties. Ring-necked pheasants, bobwhites, and meadowlarks might have lived there.

These trees were an inconvenience for growing wheat or drilling oil. Farmers found them inefficient; you couldn't keep your tractor or combine moving in a straight line to expedite planting and harvesting. And, of course, time is money. Now the wind blows dust from plowed fields, while wells pump oil from ancient fossil beds below.

■ ■ ■

It will be a few more years and a few more moves to follow Dad's work as a pumper in the oil fields before our family arrives in a town farther west, where I will complete my school days embraced by cottonwoods, another fast-growing native and the state tree of Kansas. With their lively green and glossy, tooth-edged leaves and deeply furrowed bark, combined with their availability near our home, cottonwoods were able to edge out the compact cedar to become my new tree favorite. I never tired of watching the leaves shimmer and glisten in the light or digging my fingers into the deep, rope-like groves of their trunks.

On hot summer nights, the flat, trembling leaves danced with the faintest breeze and sang through my open bedroom window, evoking the rippling of a shallow brook where they must have longed to sink their roots. Cotton-woods would spatter our window screens with a riot of fluffy white cotton in late spring, shade my room through-out the summer, and invite autumn with a brilliant display of golden yellow leaves. It seemed to me that this tree was close to perfect.

On family car trips along country roads, I would spot clusters of cottonwoods, often gathered along a dry stream bed. In my imagination, I would build a home nearby so that their shade could shelter me from the hot sun that baked the land. Like the eastern red cedar, cottonwoods are tolerant of variations in temperature and rainfall—a must for living on the prairie. Their bark is fire-resistant, another reason the cottonwoods have outlasted nonnative trees.

Three cottonwoods sheltered our home and were my favorite trees until college and, eventually, work called me away. And although I still loved these shimmering, singing trees, I had begun to harbor a secret, greedy wish for the riotous colors of an even more diverse, tree-filled autumn. As marriage and work took me to live in many locations, I continued to seek new worlds of trees. But I have never lost my connection to cedars and cottonwoods.

Recently a friend referred to the fast-growing cot-tonwood as a "weed" and suggested that it be removed. Grudgingly, I admitted that cottonwoods are fast growing and that their brittle branches can break in strong windstorms. Still, I sang praises to their beauty in hopes of restraining my friend from hasty action.

I understand that some people hate the mess of cotton that blows far and wide to distribute the seeds. But like a high school sweetheart whose flaws show up more clearly in hindsight, there remains a soft spot in my heart for the times we had. If you can manage to grow in the unfavorable climate of western Kansas, bringing shade, shelter, and beauty to people and animals there, you have earned my loyalty.

⁂

Born into a family of loggers, scientist and writer Suzanne Simard was immersed in a childhood experience vastly different from mine. While I knew a few trees well, Simard learned from an early age to love and personally know a wide variety of trees in the rainforest that surrounded her home. For many years she has been sharing the findings of her life's research; recently she has written a book illuminating more fully the entwining of her life and those trees.

In one of her early experiments, Simard sought to test her theory that cooperation was more important than competition. Her intuition, based on study and observation, told her that trees were deeply connected, altering their behaviors to serve the forest community. She designed an experiment to determine if birch and fir traded carbon via below-ground networks. What Simard found turned upside-down the prevailing notion of trees as strictly competitive, unrelated beings.

Her research showed that, far from being competitors, birches generously gave away their resources to fir trees. The more fully the birch shaded the fir each summer, the more vital nutrients in the form of photosynthetic carbon they sent to that fir. The tables turned in the fall when birches dropped their leaves, and firs received more sunshine. Now able to produce their own nutrients, firs sent back carbon to leafless birches now unable to photosynthesize. It was "as though reciprocity was part of their everyday relationship," [7] Simard wrote. *Nature* magazine published the results of this research and dubbed the tree and fungal network the "wood-wide web," [8] a catchy term that stuck.

Her research showed that the prevailing practice of cutting down fir trees to allow birches easier access to the light wasn't just useless; it was counterproductive. Clearcutting the forest and poisoning the understory to meet the demand for lumber was killing the network that trees, plants, and below-ground organisms needed for their collective health and well-being.

"The forest," declared Simard, "is not a set of individuals. The forest is a single organism wired for wisdom." [9] Critical to weaving that organism is the amazing fungal network. We now understand that a forest depends on a vast web of interbeing: a fungal mycorrhizal network connecting and collaborating with trees and plants and enabling them to share resources. The mycelia in a *teaspoonful* of soil could run from one hundred yards to more than sixty miles—if you could lay them end-to-end. In practice, of course, the weave is too tight to measure.

Five hundred million years ago, plants were able to move from their watery existence to land "because of their collaboration with fungi, which served as their root systems for tens of millions of years until plants could evolve on their own. Today, the life of more than ninety percent of plants depends on their relationship with this fungal network."[10]

In an even greater display of connection, the fungal networks that allow sharing of carbon, nitrogen, phosphorus, water, and other resources can fuse together, creating vast, complex, collaborative systems.[11] Older trees act as hubs enabling fungal networks to exchange resources and information throughout the forest.

Forests are an amazing system of wisdom and reciprocity, giving and receiving what is needed for life, interconnected for the sake of mutual flourishing. Networks somehow assess the need and appropriate timing to move resources from areas of abundance to areas of scarcity. Plants determine their own health and decide when to serve the greater good. For example, eucalyptus that are stressed or close to death flower and fruit profusely as if choosing to make a last-ditch effort to propagate the next generation over preserving their energy to live a little longer. Trees make use of infochemicals, sending volatile oils airborne to cue their neighbors to prepare for an insect attack.[12]

Trees support each other in more direct ways as well. For example, coast redwoods live in a narrow band along the coast of California, Oregon, and Washington, where they can readily absorb moisture from the regular inundation of fog. However, proximity to the coast subjects the trees to strong storms from the Pacific Ocean. With shallow roots and a height of up to 350 feet, these trees weather the wild winds by wrapping their roots together, creating a forest chain of strength.

In another miracle of interconnection, trees help to create weather. Through transpiration, leaves in tropical forests can release into the atmosphere sufficient water vapor and chemicals to create clouds, causing showers that warm the air, "triggering wind patterns bringing additional moisture from the oceans, linking rainfall cycles to the leafing patterns of tropical trees."[13] Even an individual tree can be a "miniature weather system unto itself, returning hundreds of gallons of water to the ecosystem each day in the form of transpiration."[14] Fungi get into the act to create weather as well, producing fifty megatons of spores each year that trigger "the formation of water droplets that form rain and the ice crystals that form snow, sleet, and hail." [15]

Forests anchor ecosystems and enable Earth's abundance. Oak trees across the United States support 934 caterpillar species. These tall, stately trees make outstanding bird feeders: Carolina chickadees, for example, raise their young almost entirely on caterpillars. Those baby birds will need between 6,000 and 10,000 caterpillars during the 16–18 days it takes for them to fledge.[16] As is often true in nature, the oak receives gifts in return. Birds and squirrels help with oak propagation by spreading acorns. Woodpeckers and other birds pick out insects and pathogens harmful to the tree.

In West Virginia where I now live, The Nature Conservancy is working to restore red spruce and hardwood forests that were decimated by logging, mining, and wildfires. Once the greatest red spruce forest in the world covering a range of over one million acres, these Appalachian spruce forests are now fragmented in understories and on high ridges covering just 70,000 acres. And the decline of the red spruce impacts other native species.

Over 140 rare and endangered species depend upon the red spruce, among them the iconic West Virginia northern flying squirrel. This nocturnal species is smaller than the better-known squirrels of our neighborhoods; they weigh only about five ounces and measure about a foot long, half of which is their tail. Flying squirrels first appeared thirty million years ago in the time of mastodons. This subspecies became isolated in what is now West Virginia when the ice sheets receded 10,000 years ago. Despite the destruction of so much of their habitat, these squirrels are still here, gliding from tree to tree, launching themselves from a high branch and spreading their limbs and connecting membranes to enable a graceful wafting to a new destination.[17] The squirrels feed on truffles that grow only at the base of spruce trees, so saving the spruce is critical to saving this fluffy creature from a long-ago era. In a beautiful example of reciprocity, flying squirrels disperse the spores of the truffle as they parachute through the forest. Connections!

We know of these incredible and inspiring relationships through the research of scientists, nature writers, and our own observation. Developing our capacity for listening and seeing can bring us to a greater sense of the interwoven world around us. We see more clearly how all life is connected, woven in ways wonderful and complex.

In a beautiful story of life supporting life, author Diana Beresford-Kroeger[18] describes watching as yellow-bellied sapsuckers—birds considered pests by many gardeners—bored holes into the willow tree in her garden. Of course, she could have taken drastic measures to keep the sapsuckers away, but she decided instead to observe. Over time, she noticed that the sap collecting at the edges of the holes provided a sugar source that the birds devoured before flying off. Two weeks later, butterflies appeared to take their turn at the sugar holes. When they left satiated, in came ichneumon wasps to build their nest in the same holes, which were exactly the right size for this purpose. These wasps are a beneficial insect, keeping a variety of pathogens at bay in the garden.

Earth is filled with such connections in the vast web of life, but we remain unaware of so many of them. When you stop to observe closely and patiently, as Beresford-Kroeger did, you will find countless connections and weavings among living beings. Follow the threads. You may discover very little separation of life; everything is connected.

■ ■ ■

In *The Forest Unseen; A Year's Watch in Nature,*[19] David Haskell recounts his near-daily observations of a one-square meter of land in an old growth forest in Tennessee. He eloquently describes incredible wonder and connection that appears when one is fully present to observe, amazing to even a biologist.

What connections might you discover in the land near you? I urge you to look. For many years, I have invited individuals on pilgrimages and retreats to engage in a contemplative practice inspired by Haskell's work. If you have thirty minutes or longer and access to the outdoors, you can do it now. Take a piece of string about six feet long with you to a place outdoors. Place the string in a circle on the ground or over a bush. Don't spend too long in choosing a place; just see what seems to invite you. Sit or lie on the ground or in a low chair. Center yourself with a few deep breaths and allow your gaze to rest on the life within the circle you have created. When your mind drifts away, gently bring it back with an open presence and again settle your gaze on the life within your circle. Don't try to make anything happen. Simply be there, open, present, and available. Note that this practice may not seem easy for you at the beginning; ironically, the longer you stay with your circle, the easier it will become to continue. At the end of thirty minutes or more, see if it seems to be time for this practice to draw to a close.

After your practice of gazing, you might find it helpful to journal about your experience. Perhaps you'll want to sketch something that you've noticed or write a poem about what you've seen. It's fine if nothing seems invited. Before you leave, however, take time to offer thanks to this circle of life that has shared itself with you. You might wish to follow Haskell's practice and return another or even many times to this spot to notice changes or to see beyond what you've already noticed. After his year in the forest, Haskell noted that the world held such amazing and complex connections that he could never fully know this small mandala of space.

Even a short version of this practice can be richly rewarding. On the isle of Iona, Scotland, pilgrims returned from their observations bursting with spontaneous poetry as they sought to capture and share the beauty of "their" small space that they now knew more intimately. Near the Strait of Juan de Fuca in Washington state, a pilgrim left a string draped over a bush with a sign reading, "Stop. Look. Amazing life is happening here." At the same location, I was delighted to see tiny green frogs, smaller than my little fingernail, hopping in my circle; so small and discrete they were, it took nearly five minutes before my eyes were able to focus on their slight movement. Truly there are wondrous connections in every space.

■ ■ ■

W. B. Yeats is purported to have written, "The world is full of magic things, patiently waiting for our senses to grow sharper." Consider this an invitation. We have the opportunity every day to witness the connections and exchanges among and between the lives around us, including our own. Allow yourself to become fully absorbed in the interactions between sparrows and asters, swallowtails and parsley, caterpillars and oaks, rain and soil, my breath and yours. You will be gifted with awe, wonder, hope, humility, gratitude, and responsibility.

As we'll see later, our capacity to notice and embrace the connections of Earth beings is critical to our role in edge times. As we increase our awareness, we see that everything is connected. Everything belongs. We cannot cut down an oak tree without jeopardizing the next generation of Carolina chickadees. Without red spruce, a species of flying squirrel that has made its home in West Virginia for 10,000 years cannot continue to exist. Without shelter belts of cedars and other trees across the Plains, topsoil blows away, and the land is stripped of its capacity to nourish plants. Birch and fir, fungal networks and trees, trees and birds, birds and insects—we do not exist without connections. If that seems too distant, you might reflect on the quality and length of your life without the insects, plants, and animals that grace this Earth.

TWO

Kith & Kin

■

We walk within an infinity of
other-than-human consciousness.[1]

LYANDA LYNN HAUPT

T he Noxious Weed Department of Russell County, Kansas, offers free herbicides to kill thistles, Johnson grass, and bindweed.[2] I'm pretty sure that those were not the weeds that attracted me as a six-year-old living in that county. As a child, my mission was not to kill weeds but to transplant them. Squatting in the loose dirt, I would find and dig up vegetable look-alikes and then carefully transfer them into the rows I'd designated as "my vegetable garden."

While hardly a budding naturalist, I grew up close to the earth. With other homes well beyond walking distance and no school options before the age of six, tire swings, chickens, and stray cats were my companions. I walked dirt roads, fell into snowbanks too deep to escape without help, and heard the crunch as I walked across linoleum made gritty by the dirt from the plowed fields blowing through the cracks in our country house. Sunflowers, wheat fields, rolling hills, and tiny creeks were all a part of the world I loved. Even after I moved east, it would take only one step back into that prairie view to know that I was home.

To this day, being unable to see storm clouds gathering in the distance makes me nervous, a remnant memory of the many times I watched with my dad while roiling clouds formed shapes in the distance and the air hung weighted with silent expectation. With no meteorologists reporting from the sparsely populated areas of central Kansas in the 1950s, families who lived here attended to the weather themselves, and life and livelihoods depended upon the accuracy of their predictions. On hot summer afternoons, the clouds sometimes built to enormous cumulonimbus, white becoming gray and then blue-black, shouting their message to those watching that a storm was brewing. When sweat trickled down your back and everything you're wearing stuck to you; the pressure was building. Hot and cold fronts, defined by sharp cloud edges, advanced on each other and assessed whether to engage.

In every storm, Dad was there, watching. I stood next to him, my posture copying his: erect and watchful, eyes scanning for messages in color and shape, feeling the signs in air and wind. You might think that I learned a lot of facts about weather during my early years at my father's side, but it wasn't like that. It was a full-on sensory experience; smell, feel, sound, and images weaving a deep connection with wind and sky.

I claim kinship with all of that. Yet, wind and sky are location specific; you must learn the particularities of your place. Your relationship and life might depend upon these sensory connections. Native American scholar Greg Cajete has written that in the indigenous way, knowing every aspect of our being—mind, body, emotion, and spirit—is required to know a thing.[3] That's the level of respect one must give to begin to know the wind and sky. When the term *kith* was used before the early 1500s, it often referred to this deep, experiential connection to one's native land. Somewhere in the evolution of language, *kith* came to be only a synonym for *kin*. Without this useful word, how will I name my relationship with the land I knew?

Of course, I know I can never fully understand that which is wild. Although sky will often share her plans with those who listen and watch, the trickster is always lurking to catch one unawares. With the emergence of more dramatic climate chaos, wind and sky are increasingly troubled, the ties of kith and kinship strained, the rhythms altered. And when you leave a place, as I have time and again, connections are frayed. The price of admission to deep relationships with kith and kin is ongoing conversation and connection.

■ ■ ■

Growing up, I didn't know of the terms that might have described my sense of connection with the wind. *Relatives* was reserved for those humans with recently shared ancestry. It's only in the last few years that I have become comfortable using such terms as *kith*, *kin*, *kinship*, and *relatives* to express my growing understanding of the profound, long-term, and inextricable web of all beings on Earth, as I seek to become a worthy relative.

Long before mystics and ecologists spoke of kinship, Native peoples taught the value of acknowledging all life as kin. Deep familial connections are illumined in their stories, songs, ceremonies, and daily life. Although each nation has unique traditions, they hold in common a vision of ". . . the conception of creation as a living process, resulting in a living universe in which kinship exists between all things."[4]

Professor Enrique Salmon coined the term *kincentric ecology* to describe indigenous perceptions of the relationship of humans to nature. "It is," he wrote, "an awareness that life in any environment is viable only when humans view the life surrounding them as kin." The resulting interactions enhance and preserve the ecosystem. "Indigenous cultural models of nature include humans as one aspect of the complexity of life."[5]

Winona LaDuke, economist and environmentalist from White Earth Anishinaabe land, echoed this sense when she wrote, "Native American teachings describe the relations all around—animals, fish, trees, and rocks—as our brothers, sisters, uncles, and grandpas. . . ."[6] Robin Wall Kimmerer, enrolled member of the Citizen Potawatomi Nation, wrote of the importance of relationship above all as we seek to heal the world: "Restoring land without restoring relationship is an empty exercise. It is relationship that will endure and relationship that will sustain the restored land."[7]

■ ■ ■

One way to become more familiar with the breadth and depth of kinship is to experience the story of our family history: the journey of the cosmos. This story includes galaxies, stars, and Earth; microbes, mountains, mastodons, all your relatives, and you. To explore a time-frame this vast is beyond easy comprehension. Wisdom teachers have used cosmic walks and even a set of cosmic encyclopedias as metaphors to help us scale the universe into something within our grasp. For this discussion, we'll use a "cosmic calendar,"[8] where the 13.8-billion-year history of the cosmos is shrunk to a single year. On this calendar, we'll place the Big Bang at the year's beginning and this current moment at midnight of December 31. Let's explore this "year" of evolution in which all life came into being.

Midnight, January 1: Out of the chaos comes a great flaring forth. The universe is born! Pause here to take in the impossibility of this deep mystery. The rapid expansion will be drawing hydrogen and helium into the Cosmic Web, the primordial creator of subsequent forms.

From January to August, primal stars and galaxies emerge. Enormous stars are born and transform hydrogen and helium into carbon, oxygen, and aluminum. Dying as supernovas, they give away selenium, tungsten, and uranium. Birth, death, and resurrection are ancient themes. Black holes shape the star clusters into giant galaxies. Dark energy disperses matter, and the universe accelerates its expansion, drawing apart galaxies, decreasing their destruction and enabling the generation of planetary systems surrounding stars.

We must wait until September for our grandmother star to give birth to our solar system, dispersing our sun and all the planets from her supernova body. After tens of millions of years as a great molten mass, the impact of a planetoid separates moon from Earth. Earth quiets and cools and an atmosphere begins to form. Rains drench the planet and form vast oceans. Chemicals gather and life begins. Molten rock cedes to bacteria that learns to capture the sun's photons.

Oxygen-loving bacteria and the nucleated cell emerge in October and November. Respiration and breathing now begin. Multicellular life comes into being on December 14, and the calendar begins to get crowded. Vertebrates exist by December 18, and plants by the 19th. The next day finds fish with jaws, followed on the 21st by insects that arrive and invent flight.

Dinosaurs come to life on Christmas Day. These incredible creatures will exist for 185 million years—until December 30. Mammals come into being on Boxing Day (December 26) but will not fully flourish until after the death of the dinosaurs. Birds and flowers emerge on December 27 and 28, and Earth is embellished with color and fragrance.

On December 31, the final day of our Cosmic Year, apes and monkeys will split at dawn. It will take until 9:25 p.m. for humans to walk upright, and at 11:52 p.m., modern humans evolve. We will not move into permanent settlements until around 11:59:30 p.m. The year 1492, a tipping point for Indigenous peoples and the land now known as the Americas, happened only 1.2 seconds ago on this cosmic calendar. A human life on this scale lasts approximately 0.23 cosmic seconds.[9][10]

This is the journey of the cosmos and the creation of the living Earth. Life has been growing, flourishing, creating, and recreating for 13.8 billion years. Though we will never fully comprehend deep time, this practice opens us to the sacred wonder of ever-unfolding creation that brings color, beauty, and flourishing to this planet. We see life begetting life, a continuing evolution that miraculously enables you and me to be here on this bountiful, animate planet. And all that we know of humankind rests in the tiniest fraction of the whole unfolding. We are the newest and tiniest leaf on our family tree.

Pause to take in just some of what has evolved on Earth since plants emerged 500 million years ago: dinosaurs and mastodons, giant redwoods and tiny mosses, soaring eagles and iridescent hummingbirds, pods of dolphins and color-drenched corals, fruit bats and sea slugs, gorillas and field mice—all our relatives who are both uniquely themselves and fully interwoven as the life of Earth.

Humankind, along with every being we know or have ever known, evolved from common ancestors; the story of the universe is the story of an evolving, multi-branched family. No life is possible without the lives of those who have gone before. And because we have flourished from the same source, "there is a profound unity to all life forms,"[11] a connection to, and a kinship with, every being along the evolutionary path. We are multi-species beings, made and remade by our ancestors.

※ ※ ※

A few kilometers off the east coast of Newfoundland's Avalon Peninsula lie four small islands that teem with life throughout the summer. The Witless Bay Ecological Reserve is the nesting and breeding home for over two million seabirds. It includes the largest North American colony of Atlantic puffins and the Leach's storm-petrel colony of 620,000 pairs.[12]

As our pilgrim group travels via catamaran to a close but respectful distance from the nesting areas, we are greeted by wave after wave of bouncing puffins, glancing off the water in what seems to be sheer joy. So fast and ecstatic are these horn-beaked "sea clowns," I fear they will collide with our boat. Sometimes referred to as "little brothers of the north" for their black and white, monk-like plumage, they appear nothing like reverent clerics as they frolic in their summer home.

From a distance, the green of the islands and the waters around them seem to be filled with lively floating petals that randomly take wing, soaring in abstract patterns and then in chaotic abandon all around us, diving toward us as we float closer to them. Thousands of black-legged kittiwakes, common murres, and gulls of all varieties circle overhead, calling out in a wild cacophony that echoes in our ears and resounds in our hearts. So completely encompassed by life on the wing are we all that no separation remains; we become simply flightless birds.

Witless Bay is also the summer home of twenty-two unique whale species. At first, we strain our eyes to see the fins, rushing from one side of the boat to the other in answer to the call, "There's one!" Too often they are gone by the time our eyes follow to the last known location. Then our boat slows. A humpback thrusts his immense body straight up out of the water and arcs into the air, rivers of water flowing down his sides, and then an enormous splash, water churning. This powerful being, so seldom seen by most of us, leaves us breathless. I look at the faces, each one with huge smiles of pure joy. "Did you see that? Did you see that?" The sky, the sea, the birds, the humpbacks, all create a symphony of beauty and connection that captures us fully and completely. Everything exists only in this time, this place.

And it's not over. One of the mates leans over the side, offering a steady drumbeat on the boat. And they come. These great giants seem to know the boat and the mate and want to offer a Newfoundland welcome to these visitors in their summer home.

Too soon, our time on the water comes to an end. Our captain announces that we'll be heading back; we take a moment of silence to offer our gratitude for all that we have seen and to bless the lives here. Father Gerald closes with a prayer spoken over the boat's sound system.

But we are not destined to leave yet. Another humpback, perhaps called by the prayer or her own last-minute decision, is heading directly toward our boat. We see now that her calf is with her. Only a few feet from us, she pushes the calf to the surface as if to say, "Look at my baby. Isn't she beautiful?" Then three times they slowly circle the boat, watching us as we watch them in wordless connection. Then mother and calf take their leave, departing with the pod.

■ ■ ■

The story of the cosmic path of evolution isn't in the facts, as marvelous as they are; it's in the relationships. Life exists only through relationships. We are all kin, born of stars and still evolving. We drink water, and it becomes us; we eat plants, and they become our cells. We breathe the air of oaks, dandelions, and burning coal, and it flows through our bodies to be returned to the trees and squirrels.

If we need more proof of our relationship, we can recall that our bodies contain vast numbers of microorganisms. Biologists estimate that "90 percent of the human body consists of bacteria, rather than human cells."[13] "There are more bacteria in our gut than stars in our galaxy."[14] We are a walking, talking collection of beings that influence our health, moods, emotions, and ability to reason!

Our Western culture too often reinterprets the evolutionary pathway as a pyramid to make a case for human exceptionalism.[15] Robin Wall Kimmerer reminds us that, while the Western way of knowing is to see a hierarchy of beings with humans as the pinnacle of evolution, in the Native way of knowing, ". . . humans have the least experience with how to live and thus the most to learn—we must look to our teachers among the other species for guidance."[16]

Humanity cannot be separated from other beings; there is no "other." In the sacred *kindom,* everything belongs. The unfolding of the universe does not stop at 13.8 billion years. We are not the culmination of the cosmic journey. The universe continues to expand; stars are being born and dying. We, like all life, are invited to cocreate, through relationships, what is yet to be. What will come to pass for life on Earth in that very next step? An awesome, sacred responsibility has been entrusted to us. Our work is to reestablish our soul connections to Earth so that kinship may flourish into the future.

■ ■ ■

It's not only the ties of kinship that are frayed. We have frayed our ties to kith. Although today the term *kith* is used interchangeably with *kin*, I am choosing to use it as it was sometimes used generations ago to mean homeland. I left behind wheat fields, rattlesnakes, cedars, meadowlarks, and skies that go on forever for a place that does not know me. I am living with a new family of land, sky, plants, birds, rivers, insects, animals. The trees around me do not mark a first kiss or a first step, were not planted in honor of a birth or in memory of the life of someone dear.

This land and I have not grown up or grown old together; our lives are not intertwined by shared storms or lazy afternoons shaped by the patterns of leaves and clouds. My joys and sorrows are not co-mingled with the beings of this place. Without a lifetime together, can I claim this land and her beings as kith and kin? Is it too late to be adopted into the family of this place?

■ ■ ■

Early immigrants who moved across this country did not immediately forget their homeland. They brought with them memories of a landscape that represented comfort, safety, and familiarity. Even though their diaries and letters described the wondrous abundance of life (birds darkening the sky, forests dense with trees, wild game beyond imagining), the urge to reshape the new land to something akin to their original homeland was strong. Swamps and marshes were drained; it was simply unimaginable that these bug-infested places were of any value. Old-growth forests were cut down not only for homes, heat, and passage, but also for pasture and farmland. Pigs and cattle ran wild, destroying understories that had flourished for lifetimes. Birds and animals were killed at an unimaginable rate for food, fur, feathers, or sport. Vast tall-grass prairies were broken by plows. Seeds and plants were brought to the new land and grown with little or no understanding of or regard for the impact on native species.

Is it any wonder that so many place names begin with "new," when what was most valued was an iteration of the land that immigrants had known before? And the mindset that encouraged conquering the land also permitted the conquering of people whose homeland stood in the way of what was considered progress. In *The Nutmeg's Curse,* Amitav Ghosh reaches into the writings of science fiction to claim a term sufficiently broad and shocking to indicate the scale and rapidity with which the land was altered: *terraforming.* The impetus to terraform the land has been, he wrote, "a mode of warfare, of a distinctive kind."[17]

Surely such warfare, encouraged by immoral doctrines like Manifest Destiny and the Doctrine of Discovery, weigh heavily on our collective soul—more so for rarely having been brought into the light for reexamination, reckoning, repentance, or restitution. No doubt other factors contribute to the dark unrest that weaves among us, but we cannot ignore the contribution of disconnection from the land and each other. How is it possible to live fully aligned with our truest selves unless we are in relationship to life around us? Perhaps when we lost the meaning of the word *kith*, we also lost awareness of our need for soul connection to place; we failed to realize that without kith and kin, our hearts would break, and our moral compass would run amok.

I understand the desire for a new place, for I was infused with wanderlust. I'm not clear why that was. Perhaps it was the positive way my parents spoke of the possibilities when we moved several times for Dad's job in my elementary school years. Maybe traces of this urge to move were embedded in my DNA by my roving ancestors. Certainly, I came from a long line of seemingly unsettled people, staying in one place for only a generation or two until responding to the call to move west.

Whatever the reason, I carried into adulthood a sense that travel was an adventure not to be missed. Married at twenty-two to a man who could be counted on to say yes to a quest, we wandered together, living in two countries, eight states, and twenty-one homes—with four careers and multiple jobs for me—before landing in West Virginia.

I love the life I've led. Yet I wonder about the price my ancestors and I have paid for so often severing ties to the land. Can we repair the breech to live in the deep connection with kith and kin for which our souls yearn? I ponder this as I walk the woods near my West Virginia home. I worry that the time I have left may be insufficient for rebuilding relationships with the more distant relatives with whom I now live.

Kimmerer wrote that we could become indigenous to a place if we lived and cared for it "as if our lives, both material and spiritual, depended on it."[18] It seems obvious that our lives do depend on the land around us; surely, we have learned that lesson by now. Yet the journey from head to heart covers a vast territory. My mind accepts that I am one with all beings here, but I am unsure how to *feel* it in my bones and in my heart. As I wander the land, I pause to breathe in connection and ask the trees for guidance—and then I go indoors and lose my way again.

■ ■ ■

The temperature has climbed to 37 degrees on this sunny, crisp November morning as we make our way to the middle of the Capon Bridge and lean over to watch the water rushing below. The bridge is a green truss structure of steel and rivets, angles and straight lines, crossing the Cacapon River and giving its name to the small town of Capon Bridge, West Virginia. The area was settled in 1738; the town incorporated in 1902. A look at my ancestry on

Grandpa John's side has brought me here, just 53 miles from where I live now. I know nothing about John as a father or husband; that he had died before I was born was all that my mother or grandmother ever shared with me. I never thought to ask. But in this family of wanderers, I have discovered that three generations of our ancestors lived in this area in the late 1700s to mid-1800s.

We travel farther on to West Union in Doddridge County, West Virginia, almost to the Ohio River. There, in the 1800s, members of my father's family lived and are buried. Again, they didn't stay long, as they soon joined the swelling numbers of people moving west. Yet these coincidences of place lead me to wonder if I may have come full circle. If my family passed down to me the love of wandering, is it possible that they might also have left a connection to Appalachia in my bones? I ponder anew whether relationships of kith and kinship can be built in the time we have.

Perhaps a next step is embedded in another ancient prophecy. Patty Krawec in *In Becoming Kin* shares the prophecy of the seventh fire from her Anishinaabe tradition. The prophecy points to a critical time when we stand at a crossroads, with one path leading to the way of peace, love, and community.[19] Yet, the story cautions that we must not to go forward until we journey back the way we have come and gather up fragments left behind that we will need to make a pilgrimage into the promised future.

In my mind's eye, I see the black dog tearing asunder the weaving of the world, the yarns scattered on the floor in the cave. Let's take a closer look at these threads. Which ones are waiting to be reclaimed, reexamined, renewed, reinterpreted, or rewoven? What shall we choose to ensure that they are not lost to the future?

I begin my list: Knowing and honoring the source of our food; naming the birds and plants who live here; deepening relationships with family in all its diverse forms: human, land, water, trees, plants, animals, insects, birds.

Our souls long to reclaim our kinship with our cosmological family tree in all its broken, beautiful, sacred mystery. What will you go back along the path to retrieve for the sake of deeper connection to kith and kin, whether you have known them a lifetime or have come recently to their place? What are you called to carry forward for the sake of future generations of this Earth family? Make your list. Now is the time.

THREE

Communion

*The deepest level of communication is
not communication, but communion.
It is wordless. It is beyond words, and it is
beyond speech, and it is beyond concept.*

THOMAS MERTON[1]

J anuary 2014, Matanzas, Cuba. We are sitting in a large circle, twenty-three pilgrims from the United States and Europe and twenty-three Cuban prison chaplains, together for a weekend retreat. With the help of our skilled translator, Carlos, I share this true story based on the 1763 journal of Quaker John Woolman, who wrote of his journey in the Pennsylvania colony to meet with slave owners in hopes of convincing them to end slavery:

On June 18, Woolman arrived at a settlement and was invited to speak at a religious meeting with Moravian missionaries and Native elders in attendance. He delivered his address slowly to allow for translation from English into the Native tongue of those present. When it came time for the closing prayer, he silenced the interpreters believing that, even spoken in English, prayer would not need translation.

As people left the service, Woolman noticed a Native elder, Papunehang, with his hand on his heart, speaking to a translator who later explained the exchange to Woolman. Papunehang had told the translator, "I love to hear where words come from." [2]

After finishing the story, I ask that each person at the retreat find a partner whose primary language is different from their own. I suggest that in each pair individuals take turns speaking, sharing what is on their hearts. For most pairs, they will be listening like Papunehang, with limited or no understanding of the language spoken by their partner.

For years afterwards, those of us who led this pilgrimage sought to give words to what occurred in this profound exchange. We have shared the facts, of course, but the experience itself has defied words. We only know that we were changed, both individually and collectively. And still I try: We were one; we transcended words to a deep knowing of each other; love carried us to the place "where the words come from"; the Spirit moved among us; our hearts were opened. These explanations feel both true and insufficient.

As my co-leaders and I prayerfully designed and led this pilgrimage, we had been calling on the guidance of the late Thomas Merton, Trappist monk, writer, and mystic.

He, too, had traveled to the island of Cuba before making his home at the Abbey of Our Lady of Gethsemani in Kentucky. His words resonated deeply with us throughout the pilgrimage, especially those describing his own revelation of oneness in Louisville, Kentucky: ". . . I was suddenly overwhelmed with the realization that I loved all those people, that they were mine and I theirs, that we could not be alien to one another even though we were total strangers."[3]

We are made for oneness. Born of the stars, as are all beings, we are inextricably of and within the Holy Mystery itself. Whether we know it or not, whether we live into it or not, we cannot separate ourselves from the shimmering web of life. Throughout the ages, mystics have sought to understand this communion in sacred oneness through direct experience of the Holy. In their writings they offer affirmation of communion.

Early twelfth-century German Benedictine abbess and polymath Hildegard of Bingen wrote about the visions that appeared throughout her life from early childhood. Her writing, art, and music illumine her understanding of communion. She wrote, "Everything that is in the heavens, on earth, and under the earth is penetrated with connectedness, penetrated with relatedness." Hildegard explored the spirit of *viriditas* or *greenness*, "the cosmic life force infusing the natural world."[4] God is in everything and everything in God. For Hildegard, the Divine manifested itself in all of nature, including humans. She did not proclaim that nature itself *is* the Holy Mystery, but that everything is born of and exists *within* and *because of* the Mystery.

An embrace of this mysterious and unifying communion shows up in the writings of other mystics who sought to live with conscious awareness within the sacred web, "steeped in its burning layers," as paleontologist and Jesuit priest Pierre Teilhard de Chardin wrote.[5] In fact, he believed that hope for the future rested with an active consciousness of Earth's unity.

Thomas Berry famously reminded us that we are not "a collection of objects," but a "communion of subjects." He went on to say that there is no such thing as a "human community," for we cannot live without earth, soil, air, water, and all beings. As humans, we are woven into the *Sacred Earth Community*.[6] It is impossible for us to separate ourselves.

The late Buddhist Zen master Thich Nhat Hanh termed this communion of an interwoven community *interbeing*.[7] Again, he offers a clear affirmation that no singular life is possible apart from other beings in the cosmos. It's all one.

We may struggle to grasp this awareness of oneness, perhaps because we have been schooled to explore primarily with the mind. Many of us have learned to feel more comfortable gathering facts than wordlessly tuning in to deeper knowing. Certainly, our Western culture values thinking over feeling. This leads us to an abundance of written texts on theology but few invitations to focus on a direct experience of sacred communion. We often are more comfortable noticing how we are different from (and, if we are honest, how we are superior to) the world around us instead of seeing ourselves as a tiny cell within the cosmic organism.

Writer David Hinton has posited that the dualistic thinking that separates us from other beings would have been foreign to our ancient ancestors, who experienced themselves as part of the natural world. In fact, the word *nature* that focuses on nonhumans and excludes humans would have made no sense to hunter-gatherers, who considered themselves a part of the cosmos.[8] Both Hinton and writer David Abram argue that the evolution of written language contributed to an illusion of separation.[9] Written words point to objects in the physical world, but they are not embodied. Where does that leave us in our search for reclaiming unity?

■ ■ ■

We can be transported to deep communion through awe and wonder. The image of brilliant stars in the deeply dark night over the wheat fields of Kansas has never left my soul. In August, when the house was too hot for sleeping, my parents would take me out to the picnic table in the yard where the evening had begun to soften the heat of day. As they sat beside me, I'd lie on my back and simply take in the vastness of the sky. Crickets sang their night chorus as a coyote chimed in a yelp in the distance; yet stillness enveloped us. There was no naming of constellations, no reckoning of distance. We simply took it in, and I was rocked to sleep in the arms of the cosmos.

Fast-forward to times with our children on weekends and vacations at our old farmhouse in the Shenandoah Valley of Virginia. On crystalline nights, we pulled our sleeping bags out onto the driveway to lie on our backs and take in the spectacle of the night. My husband, David, would remove the bulb from the yard light so that darkness would envelop the landscape. We could make out the curve of the Blue Ridge Mountains against the eastern skyline shielding us from city lights. Murmuring so we would not disturb the rituals of crickets and peepers, we mused about constellations and what we could not comprehend. Could there be an end to the universe? Could anything be infinite? And if it was not, what was beyond it? The vastness of it all, the smallness we felt, wordless wonder.

In his book *Awe*, Dacher Keltner tells of an experiment involving travelers who stopped at a well-known and stunning overlook where one can take in the Yosemite Valley. I smile, recalling a favorite photo taken about six years ago of David and me encompassed by that spectacular vista. It is a place of wonder. In the experiment, participants visiting Yosemite were asked to draw themselves on a piece of graph paper with a large sun already sketched in the upper right corner. The same experiment was conducted with individuals at Fisherman's Wharf amid the bustle of San Francisco. In one illustrative example, the sketch of "me" at Yosemite was twelve squares smaller than the "me" in San Francisco.[10] It is an interesting look at how our *default self*—the way we see ourselves as distinct from others—lessens in the vastness of natural wonders.

When we are in the presence of the night sky or the expanse of mountains, our sense of self shrinks as our attention is drawn beyond our egos. Perhaps we might say that awe dissolves our need to be self-referential; as we are enveloped in the larger frame of life, we may glimpse ourselves as a small part of a vast whole.

■ ■ ■

We've been discussing times of communion to remind us that such moments are real and possible. But suppose that communion was not intended to be a glancing blow that occasionally stops us in our tracks and fills our senses. What if it were possible to *live* in communion, to reweave the frayed connections between our souls and the living world? From our birth, each of us was woven into the soul of the world, and it's doubtful that we can ever be fully separated. Of course, we can continue to live as if connections don't matter, to live distanced from both our inner and outer natures, to deny the longing of our soul. Yet life in edge times is calling us to reweave connections, to become all that we are fully intended to be, for the sake of the world. Like all other beings, we have a unique niche in the community of life, "a particular potential, a role that evolution has shaped us to occupy."[11]

Thomas Berry spoke of the movement of transcendence that links us to Spirit within and beyond us. He coined the term *inscendence* to refer to that descent to our soul, an inward movement that holds the capacity to open us to our truest selves.[12] Given from birth yet covered over by life's chaos, the soul must be rediscovered if we are to transform to a new level of consciousness and join with all in manifesting the sacred Earth community. As we embrace our role as members of this community, we bring the gifts with which we have been uniquely endowed to support mutual thriving. We are on the edge; we cannot continue to deny our calling and hope to carry on as we have been. The garment is being pulled apart. Yet the threads still hold potential to shimmer with beauty and meaning when they can again take their place in the tapestry of the world. Our call is to the journey of inscendence, to reclaim our soul purpose and live in communion with Earth.

■ ■ ■

When we lived in Australia in the 1970s, I became intrigued with the easy access to raw wool. It seemed a great opportunity to learn to spin and weave. I bought a spinning wheel and took a few lessons to learn how to use it. To create yarn, you begin by carding the wool, using two brushes with strong teeth and pulling one brush across the wool placed on the other brush until the fibers align with each other. Using the spinning wheel itself is a lesson in eye-hand-foot coordination; you treadle with your foot to control the speed as you feed the yarn into the bobbin, all the time pinching with your fingers to control the twist. After much trial and error, you may end up with several skeins of yarn that you can choose to dye. If your experience is like mine, the yarn will be lumpy in some places and too thin in others. Nonetheless, I persevered.

My husband built a backstrap loom for me. I quickly discovered how uncomfortable it was to sit on the floor with the loom strapped between me and a chair—and how frustrating it was to try to make the pattern of my imagination come to life. You begin with the warp, the lengthwise yarns that are held in tension and stay stationary on the loom. Then you choose the weft or woof that is drawn through, over and under the warp. I was never able to master straight edges. I will say that my experience did give me a deep appreciation for the artistry and skill of weavers we would later encounter in Peru and Guatemala. Their eye for contrasting color and their capacity for bringing indigenous designs to life with handwoven and dyed wool resulted in true works of art.

Weaving of any sort can be quite challenging—and the metaphorical work of reweaving soul and Earth does not fall within cultural norms and expectations. We are seeking to reclaim our birthright. We were born with "a felt-sense about our ecological place or niche in the world.

This knowledge exists only within the deeper realm of consciousness that all species share. . . ."[13] We connect with our deepest essence in dreams, stories, imagination, poetry, and metaphor. We cannot access our soul by thinking about it rationally.

This journey of descent, of inscendence, requires going into the darkness, letting go of who modern culture tells us we should be. Perhaps we'll also need to let go of who *we* think we should be. There is no elevator pitch or witty cocktail conversation that can describe our journey. The masks that have hidden our essence must be removed as we sink into the wellspring where we float guided only by faint glimmers and the spaces between words.

Here we may recover the sense of sacred that permeates the world, for in sinking into the depths of our soul, we open more fully to the sacred soul of the world. Limited by language, it might appear that journeying to our soul and journeying more deeply into the living world are separate and distinct processes. But in truth these are unified and mutually reinforcing actions, a journey that has no beginning or end. Our soul is already intertwined with the life of the world. The journey to the depth of soul and to deeper relationships with the living world are the warp and weft in the tapestry of communion, a woven Earth community.

■ ■ ■

The late Stephen Harrod Buhner wrote many books and taught extensively about plants and plant medicine. In his book *Earth Grief*, written as he faced death from a grave illness, he tells the story of a young woman who came to him for help with an all-encompassing illness. As he hears

her story, the image of a plant comes to mind: *angelica*.
Buhner leads the woman through a green-drenched landscape until they come to a tall, stately stand of *angelica*
where, without any word or sign from him, she abruptly
stops, her attention captured and held by this plant. He
shares this exchange:

"What is it?" she asks.

"Angelica," I said.

She turned back, hands still fluttering, lightly touching.
Then suddenly, she paused, took in a shocked, sharpened
breath, said, "It's hollow inside. . . . Isn't it? . . . Just like me."

She looked then to see my face.

"Yes," I replied. "Yes, it is."[14]

Buhner went on to recount a beautiful story of healing
that brought me to tears as I read it. Although he had been
an herbalist and healer for decades, it was this experience
that illumined for him what I've been calling communion.

"For the first time in my life, I knew with certainty
that all of us are born with holes inside us. And
those particular holes do not come from wounds
given us by our families or our culture or other
human beings. They come into the world with
us. They are holes that can only be filled by some
wild thing from Earth itself. And they each have
a particular shape to them—of plant or stone, of
tree or bear. They are an emptiness meant to be
filled by the kindred beings who companion us on
this Earth. And without our allowing them to take
their rightful place within us we live a half-life,
never becoming fully human, never becoming
healed or whole or completely who we are. Never
becoming completely sane.[15]

■ ■ ■

Connection. Kinship. Communion. We've highlighted in previous chapters the physical *connections* of trees, those beneath-the-ground handshakes in which food, water, and information are exchanged. Ecosystems are made of such give and take, predator and prey, dying and rebirth. Over time, a kind of balance is created. No one has too much, and if they do, the scales tip against them to rebalance. If some beings place a heavy thumb on one side of the scales by taking more than they need (for example, removing a mountaintop, killing wolves for sport, damming rivers, overfishing, or disposing of plastics and harmful chemicals in waterways and underground) and the balance cannot be righted, the ecosystem will be destroyed. Everything is interconnected.

Kinship speaks of that connection—and more. It implies a conscious awareness of and appreciation for the web of life that has been from the beginning of time, a realization that we all come from the same generative cosmic life force. It speaks to the sacred relationship of all beings. Tracing our ancestry leads to a family tree burgeoning with relatives, and we find ourselves at the outermost edge, a tiny leaf. No one is alone; we each have a place in the family of things. Everything belongs.

Communion is a deeper, wordless connection in which we acknowledge the sacred woven within each individual life, holding all. Holy within, between, among, and beyond. From the beginning in that great flaring forth 13.8 billion years ago to the present and into the future, we live and move and have our being in the flow of mystery. In reclaiming our soul, we reconnect to the soul of the world.

Learning to live in edge times in ways that allow us all to flourish in beauty and joy in the midst of deep sorrow and loss will require brave and committed souls. Earth was designed for "woodwide webs" and interwoven threads. We must step up to our responsibility as kin, considering the needs of all beings, taking none for granted, aware that all are significant. We must engage in the requisite work that will enable us to live in deep recognition of life in communion.

Communion is available at the most elemental level. We consume the body of Earth, broken for us, in every bite of food we take. The essence of Earth's plants and animals become our cells. We drink of Earth, and her watershed lives in us. We are made of the dust of distant stars, as is every being. Upon our death, our stardust is returned to Earth. This is Holy Communion indeed.

FOUR

Tattered Connections

■

Our minds . . . are born wanderers—perpetual refugees from presence, perpetually paying for their flight with loneliness. We go on forgetting that we are not only embodied creatures but embodied in the body of the world; we go on forgetting that the here and now—that locus of intimacy with everything and everyone else inhabiting this island of spacetime, intimacy with the pulsating totality of our own being—is our only refuge from the existential loneliness that is the price of being alive.[1]

MARIA POPOVA

We were born for connection, shaped by generations of tribes, villages, and extended families who lived together, sharing work and play. They gathered, grew, and prepared food for all, cared for the young, sang and danced, celebrated and grieved. Bound by history, ritual, and work, the community was essential for survival. Exile from the community was the ultimate punishment because one literally could not live without others. Even though we have the capacity to live much more independently today, the need for connection is still deeply wired within us. "When we experience social pain—a snub, a cruel word—the feeling is as real as physical pain," writes scientist Matthew Lieberman in his book *Social.* He goes on to make the case that our need to connect is as fundamental as our need for food and water.[2]

You can die from loneliness. Loneliness and isolation can increase the risk for mental health issues and dementia. Researchers found that these feelings can increase the risk of heart disease by 27 percent in older women.[3] Ongoing feelings of loneliness are just as lethal as smoking 15 cigarettes per day.[4] Even before the onset of COVID-19, Dr. Vivek Murthy, U.S. surgeon general, warned of an epidemic of loneliness in America.[5] With the advent of a pandemic, we were haunted by increased physical distance from many whom we love and cherish.

Not only do we long for connection to our human kin, but we also long for the natural world to which humans are connected from the roots of our evolution. We suffer from *species loneliness* and grieve for losses we don't even know how to name. As our culture has increasingly walled itself away from the living world, we have become more and more estranged from nature, which was once our home. Our dominant western culture has come to treat nature as a collection of objects and to view land as property. We treat trees, water, and mountains as inert natural resources to be consumed. We have forgotten that creation is alive, a web of relationships between and among all beings, including humans. As the web of connection has frayed, we have become lonely people living in a world of loneliness.

American writer Richard Louv, author of the bestseller *Last Child in the Woods*, has written that children's lack of engagement with the natural world results in what he calls *nature deficit disorder*.[6] What does it mean for children to have no direct relationship with butterflies and robins, sunflowers and frogs, tadpoles and ants? A recent U.K. study found that it was three times more likely that British children would be admitted to hospitals for injuries incurred falling out of bed than falling out of trees.[7] It strikes fear in my heart to imagine childhood without explorations of and relationships to the world around us.

What does that portend for humanity? Our connections have frayed and risk becoming ever finer threads, easily broken. How do we cope when we are heartachingly lonely for the ecology that feeds our soul but we do not even realize that this relationship is the one for which we long? What does it mean for more-than-human beings when we ignore or weaken our ties to them? It is humancentric to think that plants and animals do not feel the void of relationships.

Robin Wall Kimmerer shares the story of two tribes that came to the Center of the Native Peoples and the Environment seeking assistance in better understanding how best to harvest sweetgrass.[8] Sweetgrass is a sacred plant used for weaving baskets as well as in traditional ceremonies. Because each tribe was using a distinct harvesting practice, they wondered if either of their methods might be contributing to a lack of flourishing in areas of sweetgrass that seemed to be struggling.

Kimmerer and her graduate students set up an experiment with three plots of naturally occurring sweetgrass. Two of the plots would be harvested in two different ways: one by pulling out half of the stand of grass; the other, by more careful extraction spread across the stand. The third plot would be left alone as a control group. Because both tribes followed the practice of the honorable harvest, they would never take more than half of a stand of sweetgrass. Imagine the work of the graduate students who were assigned to carefully count the stalks of grass before and after harvesting!

I have shared the results of this experiment in several seminars, and I begin by asking participants to guess which practice was most detrimental to the plant. Most think that the rougher the harvest, the more stress for the plant. However, it is not the harvest that negatively impacts plants. The stand of sweetgrass that struggled most was the control group, the one left alone without human intervention. Sweetgrass evolved over thousands of years in a symbiotic relationship with generations of tribal women. Giving half of itself away each year has enabled the sweetgrass to reproduce and thrive.

I recall this story of sweetgrass when I hear someone say that Earth would be better off without humans. It is true that in the time that we have lived on this planet, many have damaged and perpetuated the loss of species, ecosystems, water, air, land, and each other and have changed the functioning of earth systems. But that has not been universally true. There are past and current examples of those who exist in relationship with other species and whose presence contributes to the liveliness of all.

Consider the sweetgrass. Recall the low-heat fires that Native Americans used to tend the forests and prairies and bring forth new life. If each of us knew, understood, and loved the places around us, we might live in a way that supports mutual thriving. If we have no knowledge of the places and beings around our home, we cannot love them. If we do not love them, we will not save them. And they in turn will be unable to save us.

■ ■ ■

The lives of our ancestors depended on relationships with a particular part of the natural world. Our own souls were born entangled with Earth; our souls are tuned to the frequency of places that complement and enliven us. When we ignore the need for connections that seem to have been encoded in our DNA, we feel adrift from the Earth community and our place in it.

It seems that only poets and storytellers nowadays tell of the interweaving of soul and Earth. The societal norms of dualism, separation, competition, and ownership have hollowed us out, leaving a void where kinship and connection once flourished. We are seldom able to name or even describe that void, but we feel it, nonetheless. And the loss is felt more keenly for being unnamed.

It's unsurprising that we would attempt to fill the void with something—possessions, experiences, medication, food, alcohol, social media, entertainment—anything that will distract us from the emptiness. A few statistics suggest that not all is well: "The average American house size has more than doubled since the 1950s, despite the fact that the average family size has steadily dropped."[9] Thirty-eight percent of men and forty-five percent of women in a survey of 1,000 people in the U.S. reported self-medicating at least once a day, with antidepressants being the drug of choice.[10] Individuals in the U.S. spend about eight hours per day with digital media, a trend that started in 2018 and has been growing ever since.[11] Children ages 8–18 in the U.S. averaged 7.5 hours per day of entertainment in front of a screen, excluding school and homework.[12] Nature deficit disorder exists for all ages.

Dara McAnulty authored *Diary of a Young Naturalist* at age 14. A young man deeply aware of the life around him and concerned about climate change and species loss, he wrote: "It feels like a ticking time bomb to extinction. Is it any wonder that almost a quarter of young people are experiencing mental health difficulties?"[13]

We were not made to be separate from nature. We were formed *from* nature by the same cosmic evolution. The atoms in our bodies at this moment were previously in oaks, daffodils, trout, and someone's dog. And there's a strong chance that next glass of water you drink was previously consumed by a dinosaur. Earth is a vast ecosystem, and it is impossible to disconnect ourselves from her. Even in death, we return to earth.

The vitality of our lives depends on our acceptance of the gift of communion. When our hearts are open and available, we understand more clearly that everything is related, interwoven. That everything belongs. Through the web of spirit, we may deepen our connections, soul-to-soul. The divine mystery revels in and is revealed by such communion. Sadly, once the myth of separation from nature has taken hold in us, it easily spreads. We start to believe that we are separate from people who are dissimilar to us.

Let's explore one heartbreaking example. We'll look to Amitav Ghosh to elaborate on this path of violence and destruction. The story begins in the Banda islands at the far southeastern end of the Indian Ocean. There, Dutch traders searching for more nutmeg for the lucrative spice trade met the Bandanese in the early 1600s in a clash of cultures.

Indigenous peoples of the time saw land as "the unique entity that is the combined living spirit of plants, animals, water, humans, histories, and events...."[14] That point of view was shared with many European peasants and others who lived close to the land. Educated, upper-class European males, however, thought of themselves as "subduers of everything they surveyed," especially in the domain of "Nature—an inert repository of resources, which, in order to be 'improved,' needed to be expropriated, no matter whether from Amerindians or from English or Scottish peasants."[15] It's easy to see that "only once we imagined the world as dead could we dedicate ourselves to making it so."[16] And if conquest of land is your mission, you justify enslaving, removing, or exterminating anyone in your way.

Through threats, lies, starvation, enslavement, torture, and murder, the Dutch forces were able to annihilate almost the entire population of the Banda islands. The objective to conquer the land and use it for their own gain was complete. The supply of nutmeg became reliable for the Dutch conquerors—and therefore less expensive. That would never do, so the next step was to drive up the price of nutmeg by cutting down trees on all the neighboring islands—one more step of elimination of objects, already considered dead, to serve the desires of those in power.

Perhaps the exploitation of people and lands by the Dutch in Asian waters seemed far removed from us in what is now the United States. Of course, if you live as I do, in what is now the United States, the song was the same, but the tempo was faster. The most infamous example is the Trail of Tears. "In 1838 Cherokee people were forcibly taken from their homes, incarcerated in stockades, forced to walk more than a thousand miles, and removed to Indian Territory, now Oklahoma. More than 4,000 died, and many are buried in unmarked graves along The Trail Where They Cried."[17]

During the same year, the Potawatomi people who lived in what is now northern Indiana were forced to march at gunpoint to the present-day state of Kansas on Trails of Death. People who had lived with an understanding of and respect for the lakes and forests, passing down knowledge from generation to generation, were robbed of their land, their food source, and their sacred stories. The abuse didn't end in northeast Kansas. Within a single generation, the people were moved two more times to accommodate white settlers who wanted the land. A member of the Citizen Potawatomi Nation today, Robin Wall Kimmerer reflected, "So much was scattered and left along that trail. Graves of half the people. Language. Knowledge. Names."[18]

The location where Arizona, Colorado, New Mexico, and Utah meet is now marked with a monument to the Four Corners. Before these states existed, this area was home to the Diné, and every part of the sacred landscape was pregnant with meaning to them. In 1864, Colonel Kit Carson and his men ravaged the food supply of the Diné, burning crops and killing cattle. The people were forced to march from their homeland to a desolate location in New Mexico. Hundreds died on the march, thousands more in captivity.[19]

These are only a very few of many examples of the colonization of the Land of the Free. Studies estimate that in the entire Americas, Indigenous population was reduced by 90 percent, from sixty million to five to six million, in less than one hundred years.

Perhaps we can open our hearts to grasp something of the grief, devastation, and injustice one might feel to be driven from one's home and the land of one's ancestors. Yet, there are further impacts of the violence that many in our dominant Western culture may find difficult to imagine because we see land as inanimate. Indigenous people lived close to the land, and it was sacred to them. It held their origin stories and gave meaning to their lives. Every feature of the terrain was alive and speaking to them. And the people knew that the land would grieve for them when they were gone.

When we declare the land inanimate, we ravage our souls. If we can deny the vibrantly alive Earth, the breathing beings from which we evolved, the plants with all their gifts—if all those lives can be deemed *resources* to be pillaged, destroyed, discarded, and annihilated to satisfy our wants—then so too can people who stand in the way of achieving the ends we seek. We declare them savages, barbarians, evil, or three-fifths of a person so that we can assuage our guilt. Because our hearts keep noticing that we are living a lie, we must deny or dull our awareness.

And greed's appetite is insatiable. Whatever we take primes us to want more. This is Wendigo, the stinking, hungry monster of Anishinaabe legend who stalks us and can turn us into cannibals with cravings that can never be satisfied. The more Wendigo takes, the hungrier it becomes. It appeals to the darkness that must be acknowledged but never fed. For once we feed the darkness, we devour lives and are left unsatisfied.[20]

■ ■ ■

Rats! We are sitting in the monthly meeting of the community where my husband and I live and we are discussing rats! Apparently, a family—or several families, an entire village, I don't know—have invaded the raised beds of our community garden and have been thriving on our beets.

The *ick* factor for me is off the charts. Just the word *rats* is enough to make me shiver. What if they're running around when I visit our garden bed nearby? And even though our house is farthest from the garden, I imagine that they might be hanging around outside, waiting for me to open the door, so that they can sneak in to live with us. OMG, they'll get into my bed!

"What are our options?" asks the facilitator. *Stupid question*, I think: *Kill them*. Not poison. We don't want to harm any owls. Snap traps should do the trick.

My husband leans over to say in what passes for his version of whispering, "I don't think we should kill them."

"What? Are you serious?" I whisper back. Then, in a need to manage this situation, I whisper urgently: "Just don't say anything!" What happened to the guy who pushed back against our daughter's insistence on trap-and-release for a mouse in our house? And now he's going soft on *rats*?

Someone says, "They're living creatures and have a right to live." Inwardly I sigh and roll my eyes. Of course, they are. But, really, rats? Do you know how fast they multiply? They carry disease! The only decision we make that day is to continue talking about the issue.

A few days pass and an article about rats catches my eye. I read the tagline that informs the reader that rats are family oriented. The penny drops. I am writing about, teaching about, saying I want to live in deep connection. Yet, I'd like to bargain: Might we pause for a few minutes on the kinship thing, just until we annihilate these gosh-awful rodents that creep me out?

The truth is that I have a long history of dulling my senses to protect myself from dissonance. And once dulling is perfected, it's not a big leap to dull my senses to the harm I inflict when serving my desires. I have suffered for my disconnection. We all have. It exacts a heavy toll over a year, a decade, a lifetime. The price of a rat-free beet bed may be another frayed thread of connection, another chink in my soul. Reweaving connections is not a walk in the park, but a lifetime journey of practice, ever more fully opening body, mind, and soul to the world, bearing witness to both beauty and pain.

▪ ▪ ▪

Author, teacher, Buddhist scholar, and deep ecologist Joanna Macy is a hero to many and certainly to me. In 2018 my husband and I traveled from Virginia to California to attend a workshop she led on *The Work that Reconnects*.[21] Macy spoke of three stories in which we are living in these edge times.

The first is *Business as Usual*. Operating from this place, we choose to keep our current way of life and strive for the same for our children. We embrace economic growth, strive to increase productivity, and affirm the importance of consumption. How can we possibly forget George W. Bush's recommendation in response to the horrific attack on the World Trade Center: "Go shopping."

The second story is of the *Great Unraveling*, when we understand that things are falling apart. We are aware that life is difficult and getting more so, especially in terms of climate change, species loss, and the anxiety of disconnection. This awareness of what has already been lost leads young people like Dara McAnulty and Greta Thunberg, as well as long-time activists from Bill McKibben to Jane Fonda and many, many others to risk arrest to protest business as usual.

In Macy's third story, the *Great Turning*, we embrace a shift in consciousness that leads to transformation. We see traction for this story in movements that focus on spirituality in nature. And this book serves as one invitation to a *great turning*, a return to our truest selves and a transformation of our relationship with Earth.

We are living in a time when each of these stories has traction. The black dog has been busy unraveling the tapestry. His work is not complete, but it progresses apace. The old woman has not yet returned from stirring the soup, and a redesign of the world has not been revealed. We feel caught on the threshold with little clarity of what is waiting to be born. It is a time of chaos.

Chaos gives birth to both endings and beginnings. "Chaos appears when the end is near, but it also appears at the very beginning before creation starts to unfold. . . . Chaos is both the primal emptiness as well as the source of everything that comes into existence." [22] In these edge times, we will bear great loss and glimpse great possibility. The connections that we have frayed are costing us dearly. If we choose to begin reweaving, it can become a time of creation. We stand on the edge. No story has gained full traction. The future is waiting for us to tip the balance.

FIVE

Coming to
Our Senses

◼

*The Divine communicates to us primarily
through the language of the natural world.
Not to hear the natural world is not to hear the Divine.*[1]

THOMAS BERRY

We kick off wet hiking shoes, don the requisite
soft-soled slippers, and struggle up the wide
stone steps to stand at last on the tilted slab of sandstone
and mudstone that hangs over the water's edge. We have
driven through the misty morning to the southeastern tip
of Newfoundland's Avalon Peninsula to visit Mistaken
Point Ecological Reserve to see for ourselves possible sites
for a future pilgrimage. From the interpretive center two
hours south of St. John's, it was just a short drive to where
we were instructed to leave our vehicles.

I imagine a relatively easy guided walk from our cars to the water's edge, but the usual path is closed due to flooding. Instead, we are led on a trek across rain-saturated bogland, our guide setting a pace that, along with the uneven footing, tests my endurance. The air is cool but shirt-wringingly damp. I feel sweat trickling down my back, held against my skin by my rain jacket that buffers me from the foggy mist. My shoes and socks are soaked by water squishing up from the peaty bog that seems endless. There is nothing on the horizon; we are alone in the vastness. Wait! In the distance a small herd of caribou appear and are stopped silently in their tracks by our approach. Perhaps I might be excused from trekking further to watch these large mammals I have never seen before. I look for a bench, a stump, or even a rock where I might sit until the guide collects me on the return trip. Nothing. All is soggy bog. Beauty lies in the smallest of mosses and occasional wildflowers with dime-sized blossoms, but our group is instructed to stay together, and we do not pause.

At last, to my relief, we reach our destination. Yellow wildflowers grace the cliff edge, and waves beat against the rocky shoreline below as the sea summons her energy from beyond the fog. Yet our collective attention is not fixed on this beautiful ocean scene, for we are standing in soft slippers on fossils of the oldest, large, complex lifeforms found anywhere on Earth. A generous smattering of some of the 10,000 fossils from a prehistoric sea are captured in stone at our feet. Known to scientists as the Ediacara biota, these species began some 580 million years ago, when all life was in the sea, and they survived there for millions of years.[2]

How can we possibly comprehend deep time? One hundred million years *before* the first of the five mass extinctions. Three hundred and ten million years *before* the advent of dinosaurs. These organisms lived on the bottom of the deep ocean, far below the depths that waves or light could reach. Most of the thirty species in this reserve belong to groups long extinct. They are like nothing we will ever know. These soft-bodied creatures should have dissolved, but their fossils remain because their lives came to an end suddenly, buried by "repeated influxes of volcanic ash-rich sediment."[3]

Arrayed at our feet is a testament to life from time beyond our imagining. Mud and sandstone have preserved this story of an ocean floor community and held it fast through 565 million years of evolution. Slow, massive geological changes brought this tilted slab, a burial ground of mud and sand, from the depths of the sea to this cliffside in what is now Newfoundland. Jaw-dropping awe and wonder capture us! What other response would be possible? Here on this fog-enveloped oceanside, we walk with the fossils, sit beside them, try to glimpse the immensity of what we are seeing. We humans are such a tiny blip in Earth's lifespan!

The trek back to our car is just as long, just as wet, boggy, and uneven, just as difficult for my always-troublesome knee. But my spiritual heart has invited my mind to a conversation about more than my physical comfort. What is our place in this family of things from time-we-cannot-imagine? Who are we all in this *kindom* of beings, cycling through birth and death, evolution and extinction? How can I possibly hold in my mind these miracles of creation? I have no answers. Still, I am grateful to be nudged out of the small details of daily life to wonder at the immensity of deep time and consider our place in the ongoing evolution of life on Earth.

I once again hear the poet say that we need moments when our self dissolves, and we realize that our sense of separateness is an illusion. That's the miracle of awe and wonder: Our "little self" fades, and our soul is freed to acknowledge her oneness within the vastness of the ever-present Spirit. Taken by awe and wonder, we disappear into the seeing. We become aware of who we have always been, a child of Earth, held in the holy.

▪ ▪ ▪

Why take time in our busy lives to slow our pace, to allow the space to receive awe and wonder? A recent study found that a sense of wonder promotes loving-kindness and altruism, helps reduce inflammation, and improves our immune system. No wonder (pun intended!) so many people found solace outdoors during the recent pandemic. In the U.K., some hospitals experimented with "secret gardens," wheeling intensive-care patients into the sunshine on a patio surrounded by blooming potted plants. The personal testimonies of very ill individuals who came back to themselves in the sunlight are touching and powerful.[4]

A field of research and preventative care in Japan, *shinrin-yoku,* or forest bathing, invites one to several hours of slow wandering among trees.[5] This connection to the woods can decrease stress and engender a greater sense of well-being. The Kaiser-Permanente Thrive website gives a nod to forest bathing and recommends "awe walks" for one's health.[6] It does seem that being outdoors and open to wonder can aid our well-being.

But I can't help thinking that it's a very lopsided relationship if we focus only on the benefits to ourselves! Such self-absorption would not serve a friendship, a marriage, or a soul connection. Instead of walking in the woods for our personal benefit alone, what if we opened ourselves to the living beings around us? We might consider listening for their wisdom, becoming curious about their connections, tuning in to their needs, and offering appreciation for their gifts to the world.

And what about listening for the ever-present Sacred One who enlivens our soul? Many of us find that time attending to the wonder of this amazing cosmos helps to further open our hearts to wisdom. The song of the stars, the call of the wren, the glimmer of a dragonfly, the scent of pines—all contribute to the holy dance in which we are enveloped. Captured by awe and wonder, we are invited to remember our unbreakable connection to the sacred mystery in which everything is held in oneness.

A delight of this life is that beauty, awe, and wonder can capture our attention when we least expect it. We walk along lost in thought, and suddenly we are enthralled. The sun painting the sky in reds and golds, cloudscapes of which no artist could dream, soaring majestic blue mountains, streams babbling with joyous abandon, tiny communities embedded in a center of a flower, oaks in a mast year prolific with acorns: Wonder can take hold in any moment. Indeed, day after day, moment by moment, nature pours out her gifts, showering us with immense, microscopic, abundant, sparse, vibrant, soft offerings, all freely given. Sadly, we do not always receive the gift of wonder, even when it is right before us. Earth offers herself, and we hurry on past with eyes focused on our list of things to do.

One of the reasons that I've loved the opportunity to lead pilgrimages is that participants receive encouragement and space to practice seeing with "pilgrim eyes," a soft gaze that invites opening to awe and wonder. We begin this practice by connecting ourselves to ground below and sky above. Our breath slows, drops, deepens. Our eyes soften, inviting sights to come to us. When *gazing*, we let our eyes rest on what is inviting our awareness without expectation.

When we gaze in that open and unhurried way, we allow for unique expressions of beauty within each member of the kindom. We let go of any place else we need to be, of anything else we must do. We are more fully *here*, in this place. Our hearts have the space to truly see the more-than-human life around us. Pathways open between us and other beings, and we risk sharing our true selves. We trust that soul-to-soul communion with kindred beings is available in this moment.

Time and again, I have witnessed pilgrims blessed by the beauty of old growth forests on the Olympic Peninsula or the stones that hold centuries of prayer on the Isle of Iona. Off the coast of Newfoundland, our hearts expanded to include puffins, whales, and abundant bird life as kin while they swam, leapt, flew, and relished their place in the family of things. It's in the tiniest of things too: delicate plants at the base of the hemlocks; stones flecked with green marble polished by the sea, ferns peeking through the layers of stone walls.

A pilgrimage is special because we spend time in places saturated by prayer, set aside distractions to be fully present, remind each other to slow down, receive the company of kindred spirits, and are accompanied by leaders who guide us gently and prayerfully to a place of ever-deeper awareness. But travel and companionship are not required for this practice. You can bring these same intentions to a walk in your backyard or a nearby park. Moments of wonder can be found by lying on your back to observe the vastness of the night sky, knowing that what you can see—as amazing as it is—is only a fraction of a fraction of stars and galaxies in the vast cosmos. Take a magnifying glass and really look at the rich and beautifully complex landscapes in a dot of moss. Watch the sunsets. Listen to birdsong. Be fully open to the sacred unity of the life around you, here and now.

There are many ways to open our hearts; being fully present in nature is not the only way, but it is a way. In each moment, we choose whether to take this journey. When we slow enough to gaze upon the world, we are almost always greeted with gifts of beauty, awe, and wonder. We receive the gifts of this amazing Earth and deepen our relationship with the sacred all around and within us.

■ ■ ■

Here's one practice that may assist you in expanding your awareness of beauty, awe, and connection: On our Iona pilgrimages, we offer the ancient Celtic practice of *tuning your five-stringed harp*, which involves attending to your senses one-by-one. Find a place outdoors where you will not be too distracted. Sit, stand, or lie down, whatever is comfortable for you. Ground yourself there, sensing your connection to the earth below and the sky above. Take a few long, deep breaths, then let your breath slow and deepen as it comes to a normal rhythm. Relax your shoulders, jaw, eyes, and any other places where you are holding tension. Open your heart.

Now attend to your hearing. You might want to close your eyes to focus all your attention on listening. Don't strain to pick up sounds; quiet your thoughts and let the sounds come to you. For five to ten minutes, or what-ever is right for you, simply stay with listening. When you find that your mind has wandered to something else, gently bring your attention back to what you are hear-ing. We tend to separate what we hear into sounds of nature, people, and mechanical things. See if you can omit the labels and the judgments that attach themselves to the labels. Let whatever is given in each moment wash over you.

When it seems invited, move on to the next of your sense and repeat. Of course, take care of yourself, espe-cially with tasting, and make sure that you know what is safe for you. You might find it meaningful to focus on your sense of taste as you begin your next meal.

When you have completed this practice, journal about what you noticed. When did you feel most aware of and connected to the sacred? What might have gotten in your way of such a connection? What do you want to take with you into the rest of your day? On days when you feel too rushed to complete the full practice, simply deepen your attention with one of your senses.

■ ■ ■

As you walk along the forest trail, your footsteps crunch-ing leaves and cracking twigs, you alert the dwellers there to your presence. You may hear rustling and see bushes waving in the wake of a departure. Birds take flight, shar-ing with others through their movement and calls. Insects change their tune or hush into silence. Trees and plants communicate with each other, sending messages via the underground fungal network as well as through the release of aerosols. Although some of these aerosols rise into the air and blend with water vapor to plant the seeds of rain, others infuse the air around the tree canopy as a welcome or warning signal to other trees.[7]

Decades ago, scientists found that acacia trees in the African savannah immediately pumped toxic substances to their leaves when they felt hungry giraffes beginning to nibble on them. As other trees in the vicinity sensed the gas emitted from the gnawed-upon trees, they too took precautionary measures and added toxin to their leaves. Giraffes had to move away from the area or downwind to get ahead of the trees' early warning network.[8]

Beeches, spruce, and oaks register pain as leaves are eaten by caterpillars and send electrical signals through underground fungal networks to alert other trees. However, if the roots are in trouble, a back-up communication process takes over, and the leaves release scent compounds to warn their neighbors of impending danger. Trees can also release pheromones to call for help from specific beneficial insects. Scents emitted from fruit trees, willows, and chestnuts beckon passing bees. What a wonder! Communication through scent is happening all around us! Parenthetically and sadly, our methods of selective breeding for many plants, especially food crops, have eliminated the plants' ability to communicate with their kin. Most industrial farm fields are silent, easy prey for insect pests, thereby justifying the application of pesticides, the harm rippling through waterways and bloodstreams.[9]

Imagine all these tiny molecules wafting from tree to tree throughout the forest. You breathe them into your lungs as you walk in these woods, the microbiome of your body meeting the molecules born of the trees. Imagine how these signals may differ in a plant community under threat and one where individuals are safe. Does wandering in a recently harvested or newly planted woodland feel the same to you as walking in an old growth forest? Studies have shown that blood pressure is lowered in stands of old oaks.[10] No wonder ancient oaks have been considered sacred by untold generations of peoples!

As you walk along the forest trail, attend to each breath. What are you taking in? Do you sense any way in which the trees may be communing with you? What might they notice as you breathe out? When your heart fills with love and gratitude, is that message carried on the molecules you release to the forest community? Are aerosols of your indifference or anger transmitted to the trees? When the mother tree tells others of your presence, is it a warning or a welcome? Are the trees thankful for you?

■ ■ ■

Too often we take for granted what is most abundant and what we most urgently need for life itself. Earth regularly showers us with gifts of wonder and sustenance: the air we breathe, the water we drink, food, shelter, sun, shade, climate that permits life. When we take the time to attend to amazing gifts so freely given, our response is often a welling of gratitude.

Practices of giving thanks are at the heart of all major spiritual traditions, arguably none more eloquent and expansive than that of the Thanksgiving Address of the Haudenosaunee Confederacy. Known in the Onondaga language as the "Words That Come Before All Else,"[11] this extended practice acknowledges one by one the many gifts of the natural world and offers thanks to the kin who gift us with all that is needed for life. Individually acknowledging each of these many gifts reminds us that we are wealthy indeed.

From such a sense of generous abundance comes a desire to give back, to offer our own gifts in return as thanks. There are many ways to give back: a bow, a song, a poem, a drink of water, a commitment to protect. Unlike with products or money, relationships between giver and receiver are established with gifts. You feel thankful and responsible. In this way, gifts increase in value as they move from one individual to another. And Earth is always giving. You might say that acknowledging gifts, responding in gratitude, and returning gifts in reciprocity is a well-established Earth practice.

Yet, the concept of exchanging gifts with the natural world may feel counter-cultural to us. In the United States, our laws reinforce the idea of land belonging to us to use for our personal benefit. With a few notable exceptions, nonhuman beings have no rights, and to our shame, that is true for some humans as well. We speak of *natural resources,* and the language implies that they are ours for the taking. Notice the world of difference in the attitude and impact of *consuming resources* and *receiving gifts.* Which contributes to a sense of joy and well-being? Which practice nurtures us in our grief? Feeds our souls? If we were to embrace living in a world of gifts, how might it change us and our relationship with others? With all beings in the web of life?

Benedictine monk Brother David Steindl-Rast has written for many years about gratitude as a pathway to joy and fulfillment. Teacher and cofounder of *A Network for Grateful Living,* his wisdom is a balm for the soul. He affirms the commitment we make to live in communion with and gratitude for this world: "A lifetime may not be long enough to attune ourselves fully to the harmony of the universe. But just to become aware that we can resonate with it—that alone can be like waking up from a dream."[12]

■ ■ ■

With such an abundance of life-giving gifts, why are we not living in a permanent state of gratitude? At least in part, we have become habituated to seeing with the eyes of our mind. Our minds love to stay busy planning and organizing the future or replaying the past. When we see primarily with the eyes of the mind, we find it difficult to fully *experience* the present moment. And it is in the present moment that we open to awe and wonder; succumb to love and compassion; feel joy, grief, and gratitude; and experience the presence of the Holy One. When we shift to seeing with the eyes of our heart, we can more fully experience a long, loving look at the real. From that contemplative space, we increase our capacity for deeper relationships with others and with Earth.

Seeing with the eyes of the heart can be an intentional practice. We can make a conscious choice to drop our attention into our heart space, slowing to expand our capacity for awareness. Then the seeds of gratitude are planted. We can choose to direct our attention to those seeds, nurture them, and make the space for gratitude to grow. This way of being is a gift of grace.

At some point, you may have been encouraged to keep a gratitude journal, or perhaps you are engaged in this practice now. Research has found that keeping a gratitude journal reduces stress, supports psychological health, increases empathy, reduces aggression, results in healthier relationships, improves sleep, increases self-esteem, makes for a longer and happier life—the list actually goes on![13] Surely this list is sufficient to understand that attending to gratitude benefits you personally. And what of the benefits to Earth and the beings whose lives we hold in our hands in a multitude of decisions we make daily? Wouldn't that make the practice worthwhile?

Loving relationships within human families are enhanced by feelings of gratitude. Is it any surprise that getting in touch with our gratitude for the more-than-human beings who nurture our bodies, lift our spirits, and feed our souls enhances our loving relationships with them? Our souls thrive in deep communion within the cosmic family. We can demonstrate our love for the world though our relationships with specific soul places and beings. We can expand our loving relationship moment by moment: in *this* pause to absorb the beauty, *this* heartfelt expression of gratitude, *this* offering of gifts to our beloved. We can choose to repeat this time and again until our souls find their home in the endlessly flowing exchange of gratitude and love.

■ ■ ■

It has been four years since the walk to Mistaken Point and the opportunity to sit with that ancient story. The group of pilgrims for which we prepared has come and gone. I've since taken a class to better understand the great extinction events that have occurred throughout Earth's history. My husband and I created a cosmic walk,[14] scaling down the 13.8 billion years since the great flaring forth into a walkable timeline of the universe. I've written about Earth's evolution to highlight the barely-a-blink time in which humans have walked this land. Despite those efforts, I am no closer to understanding the larger questions I pondered on that wet walk back from the fossils. How fortunate that a state of wonder does not require knowledge, only the presence to receive the gifts in each moment. That is more than enough.

SIX

Dancing with Grief & Joy

Don't apologize for the sorrow, grief, and rage you feel.
It is a measure of your humanity and your maturity.
It is a measure of your open heart, and as your heart
breaks open there will be room for the world to heal.[1]

JOANNA MACY

The *New York Times* headline reads, "Congo to Auction Land to Oil Companies: 'Our Priority is Not to Save the Planet.'"[2] Never short of irony, this world. I'm greeted by this headline as I'm reading the book *Ever Green: Saving the Big Forests to Save the Planet*.[3] The authors write that to have even a chance to keep climate change within tolerable limits, we must protect the five largest rainforests on Earth: The North American mega forest in Alaska and northern Canada, the Amazon rainforest, the Taiga (which is mostly in Russia), the forests of New Guinea, and the forest of the Congo. If the carbon sequestered in these mega-forests were released, the atmospheric greenhouse gases causing climate change would increase catastrophically.[4]

The Congo basin forest in question represents ten percent of the world's tropical forests. Its peatlands cover one hundred thousand square kilometers and are the largest in the world. Together this ecosystem absorbs carbon equivalent to ten years of global emissions[5] and supports a vast array of animals, plants, and birds. Virunga National Park, located within the forest, is noted for its biodiversity and is home to the world's most important gorilla sanctuary. Bonobos, the closest relatives of humans, are only found in this rainforest. As is always the case, losing a forest would be tragic for both climate and biodiversity.

A 500-million-dollar agreement was forged in 2021 at COP26 and designed to protect Congo's forests and promote the regeneration of eight million hectares of degraded land and forests; the agreement fell apart within just eight months. The war in Ukraine and politically charged domestic issues moved front and center, and countries that have long benefited from expansive consumption of fossil fuels are promoting the need for even more oil and gas production. The painstakingly crafted agreement to help the Congo preserve carbon sinks and irreplaceable ecosystems has given way to the expediency of the times.

Short of a miracle, by the time you read this, the rights to drill for oil and gas in one of the world's most important forests will have been sold for the potential of producing one million barrels of oil per day. How do you balance the need for oil against the destruction of an irreplaceable mega-forest? How do you respond to Tosi Mpanu Mpanu, the Congo's lead representative on climate issues and an advisor to the minister of hydrocarbons, who says, "Our priority is not to save the planet."[6]

Frustrated, angry, and sad, I email the article to friends. I post a link on Facebook with an explanation and an emoji indicating heartbreak. Five people respond. Two days later, fifty-seven people acknowledge my post about a party in our community. Now in addition to feeling frustrated and sad, I also feel alone. Even my friends are not stirred to action or at least a show of concern on this issue.

I write letters and am jaded by the responses—or lack thereof—from lawmakers who don't seem to think that it is their priority to save the planet either. The deal required raising $500 million in pledges, far less than the five and a half billion dollars spent recently for four minutes of weightlessness in suborbital space.

Shall we simply turn aside from seeing the destruction perpetuated on the creatures of the forest, the community of trees and other living beings, the people of the Congo, and every living creature on the face of this planet? It seems that we're skipping along the cliff edge, ignoring the ground slipping away under our feet, while singing loudly to block the sound of waves crashing against the rocks below.

Of course, my Facebook experience does not tell the whole story. Reporting the results of a 2019 study of over two thousand adults in the United States, the American Psychological Association noted that over two-thirds of adults surveyed reported feeling at least a little *eco-anxiety*[7]—"the chronic fear of environmental doom."[8] Experts are quick to point out that this is not a mental disorder but a very understandable response to the real threats of climate change. The numbers were even more striking in a 2018 Yale and George Mason Universities study that found seventy-three percent of Americans are "very" or "somewhat" worried about global warming.[9] Could it be that many of us are anxious, fearful, sad, angry, and grieving, but we don't talk about it?

The research on grief is expanding as climate change triggers anxiety, fear, and sorrow in multiple ways. Eco-anxiety originates from our fear of what will happen to us, our children, and the world in this uncertain future. Post-traumatic stress disorder can linger for those who have lost family members, homes, and communities to fires, floods, tornadoes, hurricanes, and other disasters. Such traumatic events are occurring ever more frequently—and often repeatedly in the same location to the same people— as we move deeper into climate chaos. *Solastalgia* is the term for the emotional distress experienced when one's home or sense of place is lost because of environmental change. This may result in the need to move or to continue to live in a radically altered environment that is our home. *Ecological grief* is felt in response to climate-related losses of valued species, ecosystems, and meaningful landscapes due to climate change. This may include physical losses, loss of environmental culture and identity, or anticipated future loss.

With so many definitions, it's easy to lose the intensity of the feeling among the words. How does grief live in the lives of people, plants, and animals, hemlocks and mountain tops, coral reefs and native bees, monarchs and whales? What strands of sorrow are being absorbed into the essence of all beings?

Grief looks like the people of the buffalo when the buffalo are massacred, and it looks like the few remaining buffalo bereft of kith and kin. It rips away like the generational knowledge of rice harvesting left behind on a forced death walk from the home of lakes to the Kansas plains—and in the lakes and rice no longer tended by their people. Grief embeds like pain, whipped into one's DNA and passed on to heirs and in the land bereft of her people. Grief smells like the mud that floods your home and pastes its sticky darkness over your belongings, like smoke and ash from the fire that razed your hometown and settled in your lungs—and the forests, fields, and wildlife decimated by flood and fire.

Grief appears on the hillside as acres of hemlocks standing leafless and dying. It reflects like the Great Salt Lake and the Colorado when once shimmering waters are diminished beyond recognition. Grief echoes like ocean gyres of plastic or a whale's last gasp on a crowded beach. It flows like water from glaciers once solid, like mushy permafrost now humming with insects. Grief tastes like the grit of plowed fields that has lost the memory of living soil. It dissolves like monarchs without milkweed, sage grouse without sagebrush, and wolves without land to roam.

We have all faced personal grief. To be alive has always meant experiencing grief and loss. Yet these are no ordinary times. We face multiple and accelerating losses that will continue to reverberate for millennia. The grief of this time is existential, it permeates all beings, and there is no end in sight.

■ ■ ■

Instructions for weaving joy and grief: Take a clean piece of paper from your recycling bin. Be sure that it's not so densely or colorfully printed that you cannot see the words you'll be writing on the paper. Cut a strip 18–24

inches long and about 2 inches wide. On one side, perhaps
with a marker, write some of the words that came up for
you as you considered awe and wonder in the last chapter. Those might include words like *beauty*, *joy*, *wonder*,
gratitude, and others. You choose. On the other side of the
strip, write the feelings that came up for you as you read
this chapter. Perhaps you might include words like *sorrow*,
sadness, *anger*, *loss*, or *grief*. Again, your choice.

You will be joining the ends of the strip of paper with
tape, staples, or glue, but before you do, make a half twist
in one of the ends. This will result not in a circle but a
Möbius strip. When the ends are joined together, begin
anywhere, and read the words aloud as you trace them
with your finger on the circuit of the strip. Continue reading, slowing each time, and taking in the emotion of each
word until the words become a prayer from your heart
that is open wide to hold each of these emotions, sequen-
tially and simultaneously, even as you are aware of the
whole. This is our work on the edge of loss, to hold in its
entirety this seemingly contradictory web of feelings and
emotions and to take a long, loving look at the real, allowing our hearts to break open to embrace it all.

■ ■ ■

The death of my dad was especially painful. My beloved
mother had died three years before, as Dad and I sat at
either side of her bed holding her hands. Her loss brought
Dad and me closer still, as we talked every evening, sharing tiny details of our day. Because I lived a plane ride plus
a five-hour drive away, I would stay with him for a week
each time I visited. I cooked the food he liked, we talked
and sat together silently, and I took him for long drives

in the country. We would wander literally and figuratively down the lanes of our shared lives and memories.

When his neighbor called to tell me that he had suffered a stroke, I immediately flew out to be at his side. For two weeks, time had no meaning. I sat with him all day, every day. He was 98 and had been living alone without assistance. Had he been able to speak, I'm sure that Dad would have told me as he had many times that he'd had a good life, but I was not ready for him to leave me. I held his hand and talked to him. Yet when he drew his final breath, I was at my childhood home asleep, and that broke my heart. My intention to bear witness, to be there with the man I had loved and who had loved me for my entire life, fell short when it might have mattered most. The grief of losing my last beloved parent was layered with shame and longing for what might have been.

After the funeral I went home to Virginia, went back to work, and tried not to think about whether Dad felt abandoned in his last moments. There is plenty one can do throughout the day if the intent is to suppress one's feelings; in the early morning hours, those techniques prove considerably less effective. Months went by, months when I tried to forget what I saw as my betrayal.

One day as a colleague shared a story about her late parents, I had a stunning realization: In my desire to avoid the pain of losing my parents, I was robbing myself and my family of the memories that were warm, rich, loving, and funny, dulling the joy along with the pain.

For me, it proved impossible to desensitize myself to selected emotions while amplifying others. I could not embrace happy memories while simultaneously trying to suppress painful ones. I could not separate the Möbius strip to pick and choose. To deny grief dimmed the fullness of joy. Without joy, sorrow overwhelmed. A Möbius strip of seemingly contradictory feelings lives within me. Surely, they must be acknowledged within each of us if we are to live fully alive and present in this beautiful, hurting world.

■ ■ ■

Our Möbius strip illustrates the grief and joy we find in our relationship with the more than human world. We mourn the loss of ecosystems and species, as well as the enormous loss in numbers of fish, amphibians, reptiles, birds, and mammals. Still, we can find wonder in the day to day of the wilder world. The beauty and intricacy of a spider web with dew drop diamonds shining in the rising sun does not make up for the worldwide loss of insects in the last fifty years, yet it is awe-inspiring. Loss and beauty sing together as the still miraculous dawn chorus of birds comes alive around the world each morning, even though an ever-increasing number of choir members are silenced. We drive past acres and acres of ghostly gray sticks that were once a forest of tall, vibrant hemlocks that fed and sheltered the community both above and below ground. These trees have been decimated by the invasive wooly adelgids that have flourished in a warming climate. Not far away, you may see tiny oaks have begun their journey by cracking open and pushing through the soil after waiting patiently in darkness. For centuries beyond time, this has been the life cycle of oaks. So much beauty and wonder, so much sorrow and loss. Awe, wonder, and beauty don't erase loss, but they can help us to bear it.

Every living being on Earth today will likely face many times of collective grief. Do you sense this collective impasse, when no matter how hard we try, we find no way forward? It's understandably difficult to read about giant redwoods being threatened by raging wildfires when it all feels hopeless already. Maybe it's better to numb ourselves with shopping, eating, or binge-watching cat videos than to face painful questions about a future for which there appear to be no satisfactory answers. At some level, we realize that refusing to see what lies before us is, at best, unhelpful and, at worst, fatal. Yet it sometimes feels like blindness is the only available path to maintaining sanity.

But what if our collective grief has the potential to become a pathway forward? "What if, by chance, our time in this cosmic evolution is a dark-nighttime—*a time of crisis and transition that must be understood if it is to be a part of learning a new vision and harmony for the human species and the planet* (emphasis mine),"[10] wrote contemplative theologian Constance Fitzgerald in 1984. What if this dark night holds the potential to help reshape who we are? Is it possible to become better suited for living and loving as we are honed, shaped, and kneaded by these edge times?

Edge times shut the door on continuing to live as we have been, disconnected from soul, stripped of communion with Earth. We can only surrender to a new vision of interwoven connections, of mutual flourishing. Now is the time for reweaving connections to Earth in ways beyond our experience and understanding. Can we allow ourselves the freedom to dream of such a possibility? Dare we hope that as we live with the grief of both death and dying, compounding and endless, we might surrender to a collective vitality that in this moment is still beyond our capacity to imagine?

Doing more of what we've been doing all along will only deepen the mess we're in. Rather, our charge must be to let go: Let go of ego and the need to control; let go of greed, power over, competition, separation, individualism, human exceptionalism, dominion, lack of humility. This is our collective work. There is no clear pathway forward. Yet there are signposts along the way in the words of wise ones who have gone before, in the counsel of the beings around us, and in the wisdom that has been implanted in our souls for just this time. Let us consider some possible steps toward reweaving connections.

Perhaps no one has spent more time reflecting on and teaching countless groups of people about holding the darkness and light of this unique time than Joanna Macy. From her Buddhist practice, extensive experience as an activist, and incredible love for Earth, she offers writings and teachings that help us understand and live into these most uncertain times.

Macy envisions a spiral of successive movements that lead to possibilities.[11] In the first phase, we soak ourselves in gratitude as we are attentive to the wonder of being alive in such a richly beautiful world. This acknowledgement opens us to holding and honoring our pain for the world. Macy notes how countercultural—and how critical—it is to respect and value our deep grief in losing what is dear. This step is a prerequisite to seeing with new eyes as we draw on recent science, ancient spiritual wisdom, and our own creative imagination. This way of seeing opens the door to transformation and enables us to live with a renewed vision for and commitment to healing ourselves and the world.

Creation Spirituality as shared by theologian, teacher, and writer Matthew Fox has a message similar to that of Macy. Fox sees four paths that intertwine and loop back on themselves. The *Via Positiva* opens us to awe and wonder; it is accompanied by the *Via Negativa,* a path of mystery, suffering, and letting go—our dark night of pain and release. Faithfully traveling these two paths leads to *Via Creativa* and the birthing of a new way of being. *Via Transformativa* is the path of transformation for the sake of justice and healing.[12]

I envision embracing a Möbius strip of awe and wonder, relishing the beauty of this vibrant world and our connection to her, and encompassing the sorrow and pain we feel at so much personal and collective loss. As we hold all of this with open hearts, receiving without pushing, we allow ourselves to surrender to what is beyond comprehension. It is in the surrender to and trust in Wisdom that we sense emerging potential from the sacred source within and beyond us.

Artist Lily Yeh came to the United States from Taiwan to study visual arts and landed in North Philadelphia in the mid-1980s. There she began to work with urban and broken communities to collect bits and pieces of what might be considered debris to create beautiful murals on the walls of community buildings. Eventually she took her work around the world, creating in community beauty from the broken.[13] That is the work to which we are called. Dare we pick up the pieces of our heart as it is broken open time and again and reshape those bits into a greater capacity to hold more—more suffering, more love, more grief, and more joy. More of the rich hues and deeply textured fabric of a life lived fully.

███

A few months after I returned from my father's funeral, one of my coaching clients lost his father. Through our conversations, I learned of some rituals in his Jewish tradition:

seven days of shiva, a time of mourning in which he stayed home to reflect and was visited by extended family and friends; the wearing of a torn black ribbon to symbolize the tear in one's heart, and the eleven months of *aveilut* to mourn a parent.

Rituals give us a well-worn path to follow, practiced steps to take when our minds and hearts are overwhelmed with loss. But what is the ritual for the loss of a forest? For the draining of a wetland? What songs do we sing for a town that has been burned to the ground by wildfires or for homes that have been swept downstream by raging floods? We need the leadership of storytellers, poets, artists and musicians, our deep-hearted elders, and our wise youth who see ahead their own lifetime of loss. We need rituals that speak to our time and place within our aching communities.

Fortunately, we don't need to start from a blank page. Macy's work offers practices and rituals for "honoring our pain for the world."[14] These have been experienced by thousands of people around the world over dozens of years, and they are shared freely on her website. In one of our recent monthly gatherings for Church of the Wild Two Rivers that I lead, we explored the idea of "bearing witness." During our time of silent wandering in the woods, individuals gathered bits of rock, leaves, nuts, or branches as a way to remember what has been lost. When the group returned, we built a common cairn with the collected items. As each person placed their contribution in the middle of the circle and named a loss dear to them, we shared their sorrow, acknowledging aloud, "We hear you." We want to know that we are not alone and that our expression of loss has been witnessed.

Many years ago, Macy led a workshop in what is now Ukraine in an area that had been poisoned by the Chernobyl disaster. To this town of Novozybkov and to these women, she brought the ritual of the Elm Dance. She writes that in this "... most contaminated of inhabited cities, the dance became an expression of their will to live. . . . When I was with the people of Novozybkov, I made them a promise: to tell their story wherever I went."[15] And that is what Macy did, telling their story of loss and perseverance around the world and sealing it with the power of a shared dance.

A group of about a dozen women in our community gather regularly to participate in circle dances, the Elm Dance among them. When Russia invaded Ukraine, women all around the world were invited to dance the Elm Dance in solidarity with our Ukrainian sisters. It was touching to gather by Zoom from our community in West Virginia to dance these familiar steps in time with other women, swaying in solidarity with the people of Ukraine. How deeply tragic that the same women who had felt the shock and pain of poisoned lands, crops, and trees from Chernobyl were now facing a devastating war. More than the signs taped in our windows or candles lit to acknowledge our prayers, dancing together expressed our collective sorrow and our deep hope for our sisters who are caught literally in the crossfire of a war they did not want or cause.

We need to create and embrace traditions in our communities for honoring what has been lost in this beloved land. We will face many more losses, and grief is best borne in community. We can teach our hearts to reweave connections by opening to beauty and expanding gratitude; that will be our strength and gift in troubled times.

■ ■ ■

Not only can we weave beauty and loss, we can also find beauty *within* loss. Trebbe Johnson, author of *Radical Joy for Hard Times*,[16] invites us to look directly into the face of what feels devastating, to commune with loss and with damaged spaces, to find and make beauty. An old tree falls unexpectedly, and we marvel at the rings within the stump. A flood destroys a park, and a community comes together to rebuild a marshland to absorb rising water.

The important thing is to have a relationship with the places and beings suffering loss. And Johnson says that we begin that relationship through gazing: that slow, soft way of allowing what wants to be seen to come to you with an invitation to awe and wonder. We bring that same practice to places that are wounded. Opening your heart to feeling what comes as your eyes take a long, loving look at what is, just as it is. In that lingering, receptive gaze, we reclaim our connection to that which has been harmed.

Macy agrees. She writes: "We have to look at things as they are, painful and overwhelming as that may be, for no healing can begin until we are fully present to our world, until we learn to sustain the gaze."[17] Sustaining our gaze, bearing witness to the loss, and over and over opening our hearts to see the beauty that is also within this place—that is our ongoing work living with ongoing loss.

Johnson explains:

> "Living with the diminishment of wild animals and wild places and the unpredictability of seasons is—and will continue to be in our lifetimes and the lives of our children and grandchildren—a challenge unlike even that of the death of a

loved person, for the demise of loved places is ongoing. If your community shudders at the foot of a mountain that is being blasted daily by the coal industry, you are permitted no respite for recovering and rebuilding. Over and over, you must concede to fear, worry, grief, and anger until it feels like there is nothing left to feel. And then, once again, you set your foot upon your ladder and start climbing back up: you determine to find beauty, generosity, compassion, and community, and you determine to offer it. There is no other way to survive. When things go wrong, I must accept the invitation to meet them with inner ferocity and inner receptivity greater than I had assumed I was capable of."[18]

Bittersweet: As far back as the 14th century, the word *bittersweet* was used to describe something that was sharp, biting, pleasant, and agreeable—both bitter and sweet. Our hearts will need to grow bigger to embrace such contradictions that we will continue to experience. We will be required to build our capacity to bear witness, lament, grieve, and, at least on most days, carry on. There will still be beauty to be embraced. We will find many moments of joy, love, and laughter. We can be grateful for the chance to live into our purpose in this world that both breaks and expands our hearts.

Writer Maria Popova beautifully captures the possibility to which we are invited: "The attainment of happiness is less a matter of pursuit than of surrender—to the world's wonder, ready as it comes."[19] To honor the grief of the world by bearing witness to loss and to surrender to her persisting wonders: this is the dance for edge times.

SEVEN

Reclaiming Soul

*Darkness deserves gratitude. It is the alleluia
point at which we learn to understand that all
growth does not take place in the sunlight.*[1]

JOAN CHITTISTER & ROWAN WILLIAMS

Soul: the essence of our being. Soul fans the flames of our deepest purpose and remembers our unique place within the woven souls of the cosmic family. We might say that Spirit—the sacred animating force of the universe—manifests uniquely within each of our souls. Each of us is endowed with a sacred calling that we are asked to fulfill. *How* we fulfill that calling may change and evolve throughout our lives, but our soul mission remains constant.

Although humans are born with innate, unconscious awareness of purpose, this awareness is often covered over and forgotten. In the beautifully expressive *Diary of a Young Naturalist*, the teen-aged author tells of watching a young child bound up to his mother to show her a newfound treasure of the living world. "Throw that down. It's dirty," the mother reprimanded sharply.[2] That's often the story of our soul. We begin with that shy, small, naïve sense of awe and wonder, of a compelling interest that draws us to one thing over another, that connects us to our deepest longing. Over time, that shining star becomes encrusted with reprimands, fears, embarrassment, and confusion until we no longer remember who we are. We no longer sense, no longer believe that we are in this place and time for a reason. We struggle to recognize our place within the Earth community.

Increased clarity about our soul work is rarely attained through the workings of our rational mind; making lists and thinking hard are of doubtful benefit. Our soul whispers through dreams and imagination. It appears more often in times of silence. Writer Parker Palmer tells us that although the soul is tough, it is also shy. Like a wild animal, the soul requires that you wait patiently in quiet for it to show itself to you.[3] I'm reminded of David Wagoner's wonderful poem "Lost," written to explain what to do when lost in a forest. The answer: "Stand still."[4] What is your unique place in the web of the forest? In the web of all life? To understand more clearly, stand still.

When I speak or write about soul, I feel that I am at the edge of language as I try to convey that each soul is simultaneously unique and one with the cosmic whole from which we can never be separated. And I can never be assured that my understanding is right. There is so much to experience and learn on the soul journey, so much wisdom beyond current understanding. Yet the striving is worthy, as we are kneaded and formed in the struggle. And resting in the not-knowing is perfectly fine too, for we grow in the dark even without realizing it. As you can see, to continue this soul pilgrimage requires a willingness to embrace paradox!

Just as our soul cannot be separated from other souls, so too are body and soul one, even though we often speak of them as unique dimensions for the sake of trying to understand more fully. When we live out of tune with our souls, our bodies sing off key. Consider times when you felt embodied and in a flow; energy and connection seemed to stream from you to the rest of the universe and back again. You were alive and engaged, both unique and one with Earth. Perhaps journal about these experiences. Without trying to make anything happen, can you sense a commonality that underlies these moments?

Perhaps you are lucky enough to have a spiritual director or maybe an *anam cara*, the Celtic term for a soul friend, who will listen with you for the unfolding of the sacred in your life. Sometimes we find our anam cara in a particular tree or river. I lead a regular monthly "church of the wild," where we meet outdoors and walk in silence with an intention of listening for the wisdom of our kin. We tune our senses to try to understand more of the essence of a particular being and its unique place in the world. Sensing other souls can open us to our own, and we may feel that they know our truest self.

Of course, you may try these practices and still have difficulty getting in touch with your deepest essence; it's not always straightforward. There are times when, regardless of how hard you try, the way remains unclear. The ongoing inability to sense what is happening to our soul is often referred to as the *dark night of the soul. Dark* may take on different meanings. Sometimes it refers to the sense that all understanding is obscured.

The late Gerald G. May, M.D., explored the lives and works of Teresa of Avila and John of the Cross to better understand how these early Christian mystics explained the soul. May wrote of a *knowing* that the soul resides from the beginning in Love. One can always sink more deeply into that Love, and one longs to do so. Sometimes, however, the Love that undergirds our lives is happening in the dark, beyond our sensing.[5] We can no longer feel that presence. The experience is not necessarily negative; it's hidden from us.

Yet there are times when the dark night of the soul seems endless and perhaps ominous or painful. In these times, we are unable to envision any relationship between the Sacred and our soul. That which once gave meaning and liveliness to our lives no longer does. We cannot fathom who we are. The obstacles we face refuse to be moved no matter what we do or how hard we try. What worked for us in the past no longer does. It is a deeply troubling time.

Surely these are feelings many of us have known at some time. Constance Fitzgerald spoke of the dark night as an impasse that comes uninvited into our inner life and causes us to feel totally disconnected from any sacred presence.[6] We struggle, and everything we try is ineffective or unsatisfying. Forward movement is impossible.

We may continue to cling to our way of being and doing, our view of the holy. Yet, our former understanding no longer feeds us, no longer works for us. We cannot see another path; all is darkness. Or we may lose energy for continuing. We come to a point when the only thing we can imagine is giving up—our marriage, our job, our home, our hopes, our God.

░ ░ ░

I didn't realize then how heroic our daughter had been all along. She was only 12 when the anxiety that she had held at bay for most of her life finally took her to her knees. Depression wove around her heart and mind. As she reflected looking back, "The depression weighs you down; the anxiety holds you in place." Watching helplessly as she struggled with depression became my dark night of the soul. Her dream of a bright future was obscured for her as well.

We were too slow to understand. We imagined that the deep, unshakable fatigue that left her unable to move from her bed might have been caused by sleep deficit, or poor nutrition, or a mysterious health problem the doctors had yet to identify. Because certain of her symptoms were ones that could exist independently, they were not acknowledged at the time as subsidiaries of neurodivergence. My husband and I tried everything: encouragement, praise, reasoning, rewards, stern conversations, restrictions. We invited counselors to our home and took her to therapy, special classes, and multitudes of specialists. We tried different schools. She remained wrapped in depression that would not let go.

Desperately, I prayed for a transformation for her. I could find no answer. If that could not be granted, then I longed for a transformation for us, for *me*. We loved her desperately, but we could not let go of the overwhelming desire to help her feel better. Why could we not bring comfort and healing to a daughter we loved so much?

As her mother, was it not my responsibility to fix this? Certainly, more than one person affirmed that view, echoing the drumbeat of my inner voice. I silently asked of the critics, "How could you possibly think that I haven't tried everything I can think of?" Yet I could not shake the belief that the problem was mine.

I had built a career on my reputation as a problem solver. I thought that was my unique gift to the world. Why could I not solve this problem for my daughter? What was wrong with me? Many nights after everyone was asleep, I would creep downstairs to wander the house, racking my brain for solutions. I would pray my way to work, asking for a simple miracle: help her leave her room today. When I drove past her school, my tears overflowed for the girl who was not there, who had no "normal" life. My grief for her loss felt overwhelming.

Eventually, we had tried all the recommendations that experts presented to us, except for the one of physically dragging her out of her room. At least we knew enough to draw the line at that! Nothing made a difference. Still, I could not let go of seeking a solution. Impasse.

Over the years, one minute at a time, one relapse after another, our dear daughter was able to claw her way to an equilibrium. When anxiety seemed most powerful, she gradually learned to name it and better understand what held her in its grip. Now she courageously faces any stigma head on, naming and claiming neurodivergence, as she builds a life that feeds her spirit.

The dark night of the soul was slow to release its grasp on me. After so much advice as to what we parents should do, how we should "fix it" all, after so much guilt that I could not create the desired outcome, the healing for me began when I was finally able to hear one of our daughter's therapists say clearly: "This is not your work to do. It is hers alone." It was not easy to embrace that advice, but slowly I was given a word to live by: Surrender.

Gradually I began to separate my work from hers. We began to build a new and deeper relationship of candor, mutual love, and support. Even though she is now an adult, I still long to protect her from the pain of the world. But I am learning. This was never a problem to be solved. The only response was to surrender to what was, just as it was, and stay with the darkness until the next layer was revealed.

■ ■ ■

Throughout those painful years, I longed for a transformation. I expected something more dramatic and faster than the long, slow, heartbreaking, soul-wrenching slog. But Fitzgerald said nothing about how long it may take when she wrote, "Darkness is the place where egoism dies and true unselfish love for the 'other' is set free."[7] Becoming aware of the dark night, acknowledging that our ego is fighting for control, finding the courage to surrender, and trusting the slow work of the Spirt—this is a life's work. It is work each of us will almost certainly have to undertake time and again as we face each impasse in which we have no control and for which the solution lies beyond our limited knowledge and understanding.

Fitzgerald writes that if our limits are faced, if our ego surrenders its need for knowledge and control, then a force larger than ourselves can begin to work in us. To this previously quoted statement, "Darkness is the place where egoism dies and true unselfish love for the 'other' is set free," Fitzgerald added a lifeline: "Moreover, it is the birthplace of a vision and a hope that cannot be imagined this side of darkness."[8]

Surrendering our control, our plans, and our ego can begin when we drop our focus from head to heart and soul. We must acknowledge that analysis, logic, planning, reason, and other traditional means of problem solving, will never be sufficient for this work. In the contemplative space, we begin to loosen our ties to making something happen. We accept that we don't even know what *should* happen. If we can release our focus on our struggling ego and problem-solving minds, then we begin to make room for spirit to work in and through us. That opens possibilities for a future beyond what we can comprehend.

■ ■ ■

In darkness lies the path that reveals who we are and why we are here. Having lost our entanglement with the living world and "our communion with the very core of our own individual human nature—our soul,"[9] it is time to be reborn into our truer selves. As we journey to reclaim our soul and reweave connections to the soul of the world, we must leave behind much of what we have known. Our old ways of thinking, the stories of who we are, the attributes that have defined us in the eyes of others no longer serve us. The return to our soul requires a journey of *inscendence,* seeking to go deeper instead of attempting to transcend or rise above the impasse we face. We must make the inward journey that risks everything as we dive into the hidden depths.

As we follow our call to reconnect to our soul, we will be pilgrims on a dark path. No longer able to see, we will learn to feel our way along. As we descend further into soul darkness, we begin to sense our entanglement with all beings, a frightening potential. Humility and deep listening are invited here, as is the patience of the deep underground where seeds are allowed to ripen and break open in their own time. We are dying to be reborn.

Sharon Blackie explored this time in the underworld in her ground-breaking book *If Women Rose Rooted:*

> "When we descend into the dark, we find our-
> selves literally losing the plot. We find ourselves
> between stories. All of the stories we have told
> ourselves about who we are have begun to
> disintegrate. Chances are, we are losing much
> that we once held dear. All that we once thought
> defined us, all the old dreams. It's hard to let go of
> dreams, no matter how dysfunctional. But once
> the process of disintegration has begun it must be
> properly worked through. The old stories are clear
> about this: we must die to ourselves and to the
> world before we can be reborn.
>
> "Sometimes, that dying takes a long time;
> sometimes, we can't imagine we'll ever be free
> of the pain of it. Stay with the long dark: it takes
> as long as it takes. . . . We won't find our way
> by running hell-for-leather towards the light;
> we will find it rather, by embracing the dark.
> By exploring the fecund, loamy ground of our
> being—our own being, and that of the rich, wide
> world around us."[10]

Embracing the dark. In the depths of the well, in the darkness of the cave, we allow ego to shatter so that the pieces may be reformed into greater potential. The weaving will be unraveled so that a more beautiful and unifying dream can emerge from the threads that once bound us to a dull, faint mist of our true selves.

When we descend into the world of the soul, we are beyond not only our Western cultural norms, but even beyond words. Our awareness of our place in the world "exists only within the deeper realm of consciousness that all species share, knowledge that is not linguistic but imaginal, knowledge that an immature, egocentric human Ego cannot access."[11] Soul awareness is shaped by dreams, stories, imagination, poetry, music, and metaphor. Explanations of this experience will not trip off our tongues. We will be at a loss for bright conversations to explain our most important journey. We will float in the depths of the wellspring guided only by faint glimmers and the music of empty spaces between words.

■ ■ ■

Our soul claims its unique place in relationship with the Earth community. Our essence manifests itself in relationships. The implications of this are profound. We have known the pain of grief upon the loss of a family member or close friend. How will we bear the grief when our unique place in the world, the niche we were born to occupy, is endangered, collapsing? When relationships are fragmented or torn asunder, when the wild places of kith and kin are gone, what of our souls? I can imagine no other scenario than that we will experience deep despair. As happens when we lose our human beloveds, the very soul relationships that brought us more fully alive will also be the source of nearly unspeakable grief.

If you have not already faced such soul grief, then you, like I, live in a place of privilege. Colonialism, violence, and greed have brought such untold grief and sorrow to Indigenous peoples, those who have been enslaved, refugees, and others who have been driven from their homelands all around the world for centuries. Sadly, and to our shame, separation of land and people is a practice that was perfected in the United States. Across this continent, the land too has grieved her separation from people who understood her, cared for her, and honored her ways.

If we are not already grieving the loss of relationships that link our souls to the living planet, it is likely that we soon will be. The loss will not be a single event. A sea of grief will wash over us time and again as losses accumulate. And we see it coming. In the world of climate chaos and ecosystem devastation, we will grieve our closest soul kin even as our hearts are breaking over the loss of more distant relatives. Even when time allows our grief to be less raw, our souls will resonate with the lamentations of others. Soul grief will walk among us daily, present in the very air we breathe, shared by all beings and Earth herself.

Radical trust is required to embrace our soul work as it is put forth here and to bear the grief that will accompany us. We are called to trust that the essence of who we are is unique and important for this time and place, to trust that Spirit did not make a mistake when breathing into us our purpose. Here on the edge of deep and lasting loss, we must guard against becoming numb or succumbing to cynicism or despair. This is the time to summon strength from our deep well of courage and compassion as we face into our calling.

Some are born for prophecy or protest, using music, art, theater, poetry, dance, story, written word, or their very bodies to stand for those in this Earth community who cannot speak for themselves. Some are called to be teachers, farmers, or soul friends. Some will become grief workers or death doulas, keeping vigil and offering comfort and hospice care to dying kith and kin of all species. Others will be midwives, helping to bring to the world a new story of communion and mutual thriving on a vastly changed planet. Regardless of our soul work, each of us will be carrying out our purpose while wrapped in a cloak of grief. We will need the support of the entire Earth community to stay centered in our purpose in such a time.

If you have been aware of impending loss for a while, perhaps it is a relief to have it named and acknowledged. At least in my experience, there aren't a lot of people who are willing to talk about losses that will radically change our lives and those of all beings on this planet. If you've been unaware of what is coming, the conversation in this chapter may be very difficult to take in, and your heart will feel heavy. I cannot offer easy actions to move you quickly through grief. We are the body of Earth. Her loss is our loss. Yet Earth holds us, and our connection to her heals us. We can accept daily doses of awe, wonder, joy, and beauty in the small miracles of moss and the grand statement of the stars. We can hold each other tightly in community, helping each other to bear grief and claim joy. Here on the edge, transformation is still possible.

■ ■ ■

Kintsugi is a centuries-old Japanese practice of fixing broken pottery. Rather than disguise the break in a ceramic vase or pot, a special tree sap lacquer is dusted with powdered gold, silver, or platinum and used to both high-light and reestablish the connection of the pieces. Thus, what might have been perceived as flaws adds functional-ity, beauty, and uniqueness to the original broken object and enhances its value.

For the last twenty-five years of her life, my mother-in-law was a quilter. Sometimes she appliqued designs on the quilt blocks and sometimes she embroidered patterns. Many were a riot of color of various shapes, sizes, and materials. Every quilt block was hand-stitched together. Once all the blocks were connected, she would move on to quilting beautiful and subtle patterns across the face of the quilt, stitching the front to the back while securing the batting within the quilt sandwich. The final step was the binding sewn around all the edges—again done by hand. It's impossible to estimate the number of individual stitches that went into one of her quilts. I've read that 8–12 stitches per inch are best for quilting, so there must have been tens of thousands of her hand stiches in each quilt.

She kept a small photo album that our daughter now has showing over one hundred of the quilts that she made in her lifetime. Ever generous with her time and talents, she was happy to take special requests from her children and grandchildren. And often when we'd visit, she'd spread her inventory one by one on the bed and invite us to take what we liked. In each of the quilts, she would challenge us to find what might look like a mistake—a feature she told us made them truly unique and special. These marked each quilt as a product of her hands and heart. This was her version of kintsugi, perfectly imperfect.

Our souls are perfectly imperfect. Battered by grief and loss, ignored, misunderstood, and undervalued by us, they have been with us all our lives waiting for the chance to bloom. Awaiting kintsugi. Eager for the opportunity to reveal our truth and for reconnection to other cosmic souls, they call us to return to embrace our role in the great reweaving. It is time, dear ones, for the inward descent. We can wait no longer.

EIGHT

Collaborating with the Living World

Diminishment of all the major habitats, proxy for all who live therein, means that the numbers of free-living animals are the lowest ever, and mostly falling, across the board. It means something acutely awful, I think: that the human species has made itself incompatible with the rest of Life on Earth.[1]

CARL SAFINA (EMPHASIS MINE)

'd been in a hurry to complete my undergraduate degree with the fuzzy and (thankfully!) ultimately unfulfilled promise of marriage lurking in the future. By taking full course loads during the academic year and commuting to summer classes, I graduated in three years and celebrated my twenty-first birthday on my first full day of teaching. While I had been a good student with good intentions, I felt totally unprepared to teach. I learned most about teaching from the students I taught.

Danny, one of the students in my first class, was pleasant and well-liked by his peers, even as he struggled with the basics of the fifth-grade curriculum. I don't recall, but I imagine that I had already labeled him as "slow." We were well into the school year before one of his gifts came to light. To challenge the students who did not go to a special band practice twice a week, I brought to the classroom a large box of three-dimensional wooden puzzles; each one had a special key piece that locked eight to ten other pieces into the shape of an animal or a geometric figure. I can still picture Danny's blond head bowed over a puzzle, his focus intense. Within weeks, he had mastered each individual puzzle. When others struggled to complete their puzzle, they sought Danny's help.

I had given the class two rules for playing with the puzzles: Take only one puzzle at a time and put the puzzle back together before you return it to the box. But Danny begged me: Could he please take several apart at once, mix the pieces, and try to put them all back together. With reluctance and skepticism, I acquiesced to his request. It was an incredible learning experience for me. Heretofore, I thought that being "school smart" was an indicator of one's overall intelligence. Yet here was Danny, taking apart a dozen three-dimensional puzzles, mixing all the pieces, and solving each one well before the bell signaled an end to the period. He had a way of seeing in 3-D that went far beyond the view possessed by the rest of us. In this domain, he had intelligence to spare!

As the year progressed, I noticed that some students could draw almost anything, while others struggled. One boy who had major developmental delays could play a song on the piano after hearing it only once, although he would never learn to read music. Humor developed differently for the children in this class; some would get a joke instantly or eagerly participate in witty word play, while others required an explanation. Some fifth graders showed great empathy; others, not so much. I learned from my class that intelligence is not one-size-fits-all. It seemed that I hadn't known much about intelligence at all.

Thirteen years after my experience in that fifth-grade classroom, Harvard education professor Howard Gardner published his theory outlining multiple, relatively discrete, intellectual capacities held by individuals.[2] In his model, types of intelligence included intellectual, logical-mathematical, spatial, musical, interpersonal, intra-personal and bodily-kinesthetic. Later, he would add other categories, including naturalist and existential. Gardner's work held the potential to alter my teaching, but by the time I read it, I'd taught in public schools for a decade, dedicated four more years to teaching pre- and in-service teachers at the university level, and had moved on to a new career.

I'm sure that teachers today have a broader and more nuanced understanding of human intelligence, yet there is so much more that awaits our understanding. Our knowledge of the wisdom held by our kin in the living world is even more limited. From the time of Aristotle until the present, a central premise in Western philosophical thought has been that humans alone possess a "rational soul," or mind, that is connected to the divine, and thus we may consider ourselves above other forms of life. For French philosopher René Descartes, writing in the 1600s, the *Great Chain of Being*, as he termed it, demonstrated a dichotomy between unthinking matter—minerals, plants, animals, and the human body—and the "pure, thinking mind (the exclusive province of humans and God)."[3] Descartes also pronounced humans the only beings able to *feel* their own bodily sensations, and thus he argued that we should have no hesitation to exploit animals to meet our needs. Sadly, the shrieks of animals upon whom he and his team performed ghastly, painful experiments did nothing to shake his certainty in his theory.

This hierarchy of intellectual superiority, this cultural construct of human exceptionalism, has led—and continues to lead—to tragic results for the beings of this world, as well as great loneliness, heartache, and loss for humankind. This view was not universally embraced by all cultures nor was it prevalent. Long before Aristotle placed humans next to God, Native peoples held a *kincentric* view, understanding other species and the land itself as relatives with inherent wisdom often beyond that of humans. After all, they had been on Earth far longer than we humans.

Why does the paradigm of human superiority still hold sway in our Western culture? Have we not observed and *proven* time and again that more than the human world is steeped in intelligence? Look at just a few examples:

- Slime mold can solve a complex maze.

- The photoreceptors in the leaves of plants recognize if you are standing next to them.

- Using high-pitched chirps, prairie dogs describe to each other the species, size, shape, color, and speed of an intruder.

- Crows have learned to drop nuts on the roadway and wait for cars to drive over the nuts to crack them open. Sometimes they stage this event at an intersection and then wait for the light to change to retrieve the nutmeat.

- Trees share information about invading insects, allowing their neighbors time to prepare a chemical repellent.

- Photosynthesis. Plants create sugar for energy out of sunlight.

Environmentalist D.J. White tells of a job early in his career that consisted mainly of running visual acuity trials with a dolphin at the University of Hawaii. Alone in a small tank, the dolphin was required to push the correct color paddle to hear a certain "woo-woo" sound and receive a herring that D. J. would lob into the pool. Supposedly hidden behind a plywood box, D. J. was able to witness the results by peering through a five-inch by five-inch cut in the wall. It wasn't long before the dolphin took over the game. She would consistently give the correct response, receive each reward of a herring, and stockpile them at the bottom of the pool. When she had a large mound of fish, she would thereafter get every answer wrong, one hundred percent of the time. Each time she answered incorrectly, she'd pick up a fish, cock her rostrum back, and wing a fish through the observation hole hitting D. J. in the head. Time and again she would do this. Tired of being hit, D. J. would try pausing for varying intervals of time before hitting the buzzer to signal the incorrect response. She would wait, too, holding the fish until D. J., required to follow the protocol of the experiment, would eventually hit the buzzer. Smack! Another herring hits the mark![4]

In a recent podcast, White shared other examples of his time in the tank with this dolphin, sometimes being scanned by her sonar, other times being brought by her to the center of the tank where the dolphin would raise them both out of the water for suspended moments of breathing together. I dare you to listen to his stories and try to imagine that these are not beings of great intelligence and feeling. It is heartbreaking to remember that dolphins are intensely social beings who cover vast territories of the ocean in pods. They were never intended to swim alone in a small tank in solitary confinement. We desperately need to connect with the wisdom and grace of these beings who know water in ways we will never understand.

White went on to cofound Greenpeace, an organization to which I stopped contributing in the 1980s, when I felt it was too radical for my way of addressing the climate problem. Now I begin to understand. Once you *know* that other beings are not *others*, don't you have to lay everything on the line to fight for their lives?

If intelligence is the "ability to learn or understand or to deal with new or trying situations," as defined by Merriam-Webster, surely plants and animals have proven their intelligence over and over. They could not have survived otherwise. Yet in the very way we define nature, we hold her at a distance: *independent of human activities; existing without human beings or civilization.* Our language repeats the refrain of "othering." Of course, were we to fully embrace kinship with all beings, we would have to alter deeply ingrained habits and give up long-standing privilege. Could it be that we avoid certain information to forestall radical changes to our comfortable lives?

"Otherness" provides a convenient cover for greed and ego. Author David Abram names human exceptionalism as a tool we have used to explain away our behavior: "One had only to demonstrate that these others were not *fully* human, or were 'closer to the animals,' in order to establish one's right of dominion."[5]

Amitav Ghosh elaborates on how viewing humans as superior to nature in Europe in the 1600s led to labeling those who believed in the aliveness of all beings as "brutes" or "savages." Creating a distinction between exceptional, educated, upper-class European men who were considered close to God, and "savages"—Indigenous peoples, Africans, peasants, and witches—paved the way for the "brutes" to be removed from their land, suppressed, burned at the stake, or otherwise dispatched without compunction. And with their removal, the way opened for claiming and ultimately terraforming the land, bending it to the desire of these conquerors.[6] After all, nature was not alive, so the loss of plants, animals, water, and land was of no consequence; it was surely *intended* for use by the exceptional humans.

But what if we were wrong? Ghosh responds:

"It is now beyond dispute, I think, that the Western scientists, philosophers, and intellectuals who believed that non-White peoples were by nature brutish, lacking in sensibility, and effectively mute were profoundly and utterly wrong. What, then, if they were wrong also about the inertness and brute materiality of what they called 'Nature'? What if it was the people who were regarded by elite Westerners as brutes and savages—the people who could see signs of vitality, life and meaning in beings of many other kinds—who were right all along? What if the idea that the Earth teems with other beings who act, communicate, tell stories, and make meaning is taken seriously?"[7]

What if? As we accept that non-humans are intelligent, solve problems, communicate, and care for others, perhaps the concept of human exceptionalism will loosen its hold on us. And when we communicate wordlessly with nonhumans, we open the door to receiving the gifts of their wisdom that surpasses our own limitations.

One example of communication involves two of my favorite authors and an Alaskan brown bear. Kathleen Dean Moore writes of a time that Robin Wall Kimmerer visited Moore's cabin in southeast Alaska. Setting off for an afternoon walk on a path framed by a tunnel of alders, the women constantly raised their voices to ensure that bears who frequented the nearby salt marsh would be aware of their presence. After a time, the trail broke through the trees to a view of waves and rocks; Robin stopped. "I don't feel comfortable going any further. I feel that the bears are not welcoming us." A member of the Bear Clan of the Potawatomi people, Robin is deeply aware of forest life.

Back they turned, retracing their steps until their path joined a smaller path to the cabin. Blocking their way home stood a very large bear. He swung his head around to look at the women. Robin began speaking to him in the Potawatomi language. He turned his eyes away but did not budge. "Shall I sing to him?" Robin whispered. "I know his song." And she did. When the song was finished, the bear dropped his head and began to graze again, signaling the women that they were free to pass. Arriving safely back at the cabin, the women sank to the floor of the porch in grateful relief and exhaustion. Looking through the hemlocks at the broad back of the brown bear, they sang to him in gratitude for their safe passage.[8]

Perhaps we prefer spoken and written language because it sets us apart. Consider how much time we spend thinking about words—an irony for me to point out, as that's exactly what I'm doing to try to describe this cultural preference. As you prepare for an important presentation or an encounter with a neighbor you find challenging, do you labor over individual words, hoping to craft the message in a way that will achieve your goals? We feel that getting just the right word is critical to our message. Yet psychologists have shown that tone and nonverbal communication convey far more information than words alone. We witness an individual overcome by grief, and tears come to our eyes. The sound and sight of people fully engaged in laughter evokes laughter in us even when we did not hear the joke. We look into the eyes of those we love, and wordless worlds pass between us. Messages are regularly sent and received between humans and their canine and feline companions: I'm hungry. I need to go out. Give me attention. Experience tells us over and over that we do communicate beyond words. The deepest and most profound level of communication is communion: heart to heart, soul to soul, wordless.

We have prized the wisdom of our rational minds over our empathetic hearts. We have focused on what sets us apart rather than what we hold in common; we have prioritized the wants of the individual over the needs of the whole. Underlying the twin threats of biodiversity loss and climate chaos are the lies that elite Western society has been perpetuating for at least four hundred years. The story of separation has permeated all we have known in our lifetimes and woven itself into our beliefs and actions.

Replacing that story with a story of oneness and belonging with all beings will be as terrifying and culturally wrenching as it is promising. Even now, the idea that we can collaborate with other species to cocreate a future may seem to be a fairy tale. Paradigms do not give up their holds willingly; stories and habits of the mind are notoriously difficult to change. We will have to relentlessly replace the *othering* thoughts and language that are woven into life; indeed, we must give up our way of life. Perhaps it is small comfort to note that such change is already being forced upon us in the face of loss—and change will only accelerate in our lifetimes, no matter how short.

I understand the urge to seek shelter, arm the battlements, and pull up the drawbridge. No doubt many will try this approach, and perhaps there are times that we all will. But the way of thinking that brought us to the destruction of much that has provided for our collective survival. So many already have experienced devastating losses, and the cliff edge is crumbling rapidly. We cannot save all, and certainly we cannot save our current way of living. The time has come to reinvent ourselves, to become adaptable and collaborative, co-creating a world in which all may flourish.

Thomas Berry explored this imperative to reinvent ourselves at the species level. He felt that it would not be sufficient for a few visionaries to draw from the depths of their souls to embrace a changing future. Berry wrote that we each carry within us a unique expression of the numinous mystery, and the world demands a response that "rises from the wild unconscious depths of the human soul" of each of us.[9] Thus, we have an obligation to explore beyond words. We are called to story, dreams, music, art, impressions, and nudges. We cannot live and thrive in these uncertain times with the mainstream habits of thinking and being that most of us have followed thus far. We must step into a world unguided by expertise, knowledge, or rational thinking. We will need the wisdom of all beings. In this there is good news: Our souls are equipped to connect to the wisdom of the timeless unknown and other souls, to follow glimmers and metaphors, and to be nourished by myth and mystery. Our rational minds may resist the unknown; our souls know that liveliness thrives in that realm.

How is it possible to work toward a future that we cannot understand and for which no experience has prepared us as we face this incredible challenge? It certainly will not be possible from the paradigm of human exceptionalism.

■ ■ ■

Eliminating those pesky sparrows that were eating rice and seeds in the fields must have seemed a stroke of genius to Chinese officials in 1958. Launching the "Kill a Sparrow" crusade as part of the Great Leap Forward economic campaign would surely result in more food for the people.[10] Urged on by officials, the public united in tearing down the nests of sparrows, breaking their eggs, killing fledglings, and shooting the adults.

One flock of frightened sparrows sought sanctuary on the grounds of the Polish Embassy. Bands of Chinese citizens—in what must have been a surreal and heart-breaking scene—surrounded the building, drumming pots and pans around the clock until the exhausted birds simply fell from the trees, dead. During the first two years of the campaign, the people killed one billion sparrows.

Despite the apparent success of this campaign, the food supply rapidly decreased. Crops were decimated by swarms of locusts, their burgeoning numbers enabled by the elimination of a natural predator: sparrows. The campaign was eventually halted, but not before millions of people starved to death in the Great Chinese Famine. The government was forced to import sparrows from the Soviet Union to rebalance the ecosystem it had destroyed.

Before leaping to assumptions of superiority over Chinese officials, let's pause. Although saving people from starvation is a good intention, it is not a predictor of positive outcomes.

Deep inside a frozen arctic mountain in Norway is the Doomsday Vault. Built to store seeds from all over the world, the vault acts as a kind of back-up system for Earth's plant resources. Security is tight; the seeds are never removed or tested. There are over one thousand seed banks all over the world, built to preserve plant biodiversity against an uncertain future.[11] However, Mohawk seed keeper Rowan White cautions that frozen-in-time seeds may not be viable when they are called to awaken in a vastly changed world.[12] Seeds, she reminds us, are living beings. They belong with the soil, growing and changing along with the greater web of life, saved from generation to generation by people who honor this life-renewing process.

Her words nudge me awake. My view has been human-centric, thinking that of course it makes sense to preserve seeds until a time when we might need them. Until I heard White, I did not pause to ask, "What would a seed want? What would support her vitality?" When we fail to listen to the wisdom of a seed, the solutions we invent risk falling short, sometimes disastrously.

Another example: Many industrial-scale foresters have firmly held to a paradigm of competition among trees, believing that light and resources are scarce commodities that must be allocated. Therefore, less valuable trees must be sacrificed for the good of higher quality trees. With that assumption, it made sense to cut down birch trees so that the more highly prized Douglas firs would receive more sunlight and thrive. However, you may recall from an earlier discussion that the research of scientist Suzanne Simard made clear that birch and fir are in fact collaborators; they grow best in each other's company, sharing sunlight and water and exchanging nutrients.[13] For trees, as for humans, if you lose your life partner, your own health is at greater risk. Simard grew up among the trees, observing them closely. She was willing to challenge popular wisdom and study the intelligence of the trees themselves.

▪ ▪ ▪

Autumn has stripped the petals from the coneflowers, so sparrows are easier to spot outside the window where I sit with my morning coffee. Little ones hop between seed heads and nourishment they find on the ground. The tiniest bit of research tells me that there are far more species of sparrows than I'd ever imagined and that all of them are singers. Do you have to plug your ears to kill a bird in mid-song? What steeling of the senses is required to ignore the distress cries of the parents as you rip their fledglings from the nest? I try to imagine; and then I try not to. The Bible tells us that not one sparrow is forgotten by God. Alas, I long to forget the fallen.

I claim no moral high ground here. I have failed time and again to listen to the lives around me, failed to appreciate their intelligence, and never dreamed of collaborating with them. For decades, I tilled our garden and left the soil bare over winter to the detriment of life underground. For far too long, our family raked or blew the leaves from our yard, unaware that we were destroying the winter homes of Luna moths, spotted salamanders, wood frogs and American bumble bees.[14] We thought our lawns would be more attractive if we eliminated that "weed," the dandelion, unaware that we were denying the bees their first food in spring.

When time came to replace a dead tree in our yard, I choose a gingko because of its lovely shape and shimmering leaves. I didn't understand that trees are a critical food source for the larval stage of beneficial insects. Oaks host 557 species of caterpillars that are food for the fledgling birds of the mid-Atlantic. The number of species of caterpillars hosted by the gingko? Zero.[15]

When we are ignorant of our more-than-human neighbors and their place in the family of things, even well-intentioned actions may produce disastrous results. Yes, we are called to action, but we cannot continue to sacrifice billions of sparrows, seeds, trees, and birds to our learning curve when we move with haste and good intentions while failing to listen to the needs and intelligence of other beings. So many of the ways we hoped to support life have fallen short or brought unintended but deadly consequences. It is heartbreaking to realize that our hard-earned knowledge and good intentions are woefully insufficient. The litany of challenges we face today—climate chaos, loss of species and biodiversity, ecosystem destruction, climate injustice—understandably drives a sense of urgency. Yet these complex, interwoven issues cannot be addressed with our well-honed, problem-solving *superior* mindset; our intelligence is insufficient to the task.

Before we offer our support to this Earth, we must dedicate ourselves to increased awareness of the lives around us. But more than that, we must learn from them. It is our task to garner wisdom from the living world in which we are inextricably woven. Our challenge is to embrace a new-yet-ancient rhythm of deep listening as a prerequisite for creative collaboration with all life. In every forest, valley, mountain, and waterway on this green-blue planet, countless lives—human and more than human—hang in the balance.

■ ■ ■

My neighbors are out this morning picking up earthworms. It's not a fishing trip that has drawn them to this work. It's a rescue mission. Last night's rain has filled the worm burrows with water, forcing them to the surface to breathe. Their exit strategy no doubt enabled them to evolve and thrive until humans intervened with sidewalks. Now good-hearted members of our community are coming to the aid of these climate refugees by returning them to earth. Not all rescues will be successful, but perhaps some will. And it's in our best interest too. We have been collaborating with the worms for five years in hopes of transforming clay and dirt, compacted by heavy equipment and building materials, into living soil.

It's been a collaborative effort to get the worms to settle here. In the first year we tried planting daikon radishes

of kimchi fame. Despite their reputation as deep diggers
and soil aerators, they struggled mightily, the bulk of their
white taproots bulging above the ground. We covered bare
areas with a layer of home-grown compost, added card-
board, and then topped it with more compost to create a
tasty sandwich fit for earthworm consumption. We planted
legumes to fix nitrogen in the soil, added native plants, and
overwintered with cover crops to ensure that the soil was
not left bare. After our efforts to make a happy home for
earthworms, you can see why we didn't want to leave them
to roast in the early morning sun.

Of course, it wasn't just earthworms we wanted to
attract. We were inviting the entire community of builders
who turn dead and dusty dirt into living soil that supports
healthy food for a variety of beings, captures storm water,
and sequesters carbon. There is more life in one teaspoon
of healthy garden soil than there are humans on Earth:
"one billion bacteria, several yards of fungal filaments, several thousand protozoa, and scores of nematodes"[16]—and
earthworms. In this web of relationships, the roots of plants
converse with fungi by sending chemical messages through
the soil; they entangle, and the plants exchange sugars for
minerals foraged and mined by the fungi. It is a complex,
living system and the healthier the system, the more nutri-
tious the food that is produced by the plants we all eat.

Because we contributed to the loss of soil as we built
our homes, it's our responsibility to help to restore this
web of life. We could purchase bags of topsoil from the
local big box store, but secured in plastic bags, it would
be woefully short on lifeforms. Despite all our intelligence,
we could not possibly develop living soil on our own. But
we can assist; we can cocreate with the living world. And
we can further help by restoring native trees and plants

that may ultimately support the development of eco-systems that feed and shelter native bees and butterflies, moths and dragonflies, chickadees and bluebirds, frogs and owls. Each life creates conditions conducive to life in an intelligent world.

■ ■ ■

Janine Benyus pioneered the concept of biomimicry, the conscious emulation of life's genius—not learning *about* nature, learning *from* nature. We are, Benyus says, here to be the helpers of the helpers, not the managers. It's our work to "set a banquet," for the real helpers, to help create the conditions conducive to life so that life can heal herself.[17] Sit with that a bit. In truth, we will never develop the intelligence needed to supply technological solutions to the twin challenges of climate chaos and biodiversity loss. And that is not ours to do; others of our kin have already proven their capacity for bringing renewal and vitality to places that have been devastated. Our calling is to help the helpers. To observe, listen, become curious, and ask, "What would nature do here? How can I help?"

The YouTube video *How Wolves Change Rivers* received 44 million views in the last nine years, so it's likely you have seen it. It's an incredible story of reintroducing wolves to Yellowstone National Park, which changed the behavior of deer, which in turn accelerated the growth of trees, the return of birds, and the reintroduction of beavers whose dams provided habitats for otters, muskrats, ducks, fish, reptiles, and amphibians. The wolves killed coyotes, increasing the number of rabbits and mice and resulting in more hawks, weasels, foxes, and badgers. The effects continued until the flow of the rivers was changed by the regeneration of forests. If you haven't watched it, or even if you have, follow the link in the endnotes.[18] It's a beautiful example of how each species offers its specific contribution until ultimately the whole is larger than the parts. It's also very clear that this complex interaction of events is far beyond what human engineering could accomplish; the role of people was to reintroduce the wolves and thereby help the helpers.

Another example is the work of beavers, the masters of water flow. They build systems that store water in advance of droughts, slow and spread streams to avoid flooding, create thriving wetlands, recharge the groundwater, serve as firebreaks, and create habitat for fish, turtles, birds, and other life. It is estimated that before European contact on this continent, beaver dams stored an additional 230,000 square miles of water, the equivalent area of Arizona and New Mexico combined. Think how that would have changed the dynamic for the now deeply thirsty American west. However, at that time, there were about four hundred million beavers. Today there are between ten and fifteen million. Seen by trappers, traders, and settlers as a commodity or a nuisance, beavers were killed for their pelts and oil glands or to eliminate their impact, leaving lands and life longing for water.[19]

Today we know that beavers are a keystone species. Like the stone in the top of an arch that holds all the other stones in place, keystone species are critical to the life of many others. Of course, if you remove the keystone, the system collapses. For example, consider those wetlands that beavers create. Wetlands in the United States make up only twenty-two percent of the land—and eighty percent of our biodiversity. Help the helpers. Return beavers, and other life finds a home.

The Occidental Arts & Ecology Center in Sonoma County California is working to do just that. With ranchers, it explores strategies for coexistence and collaboration. Running a pipe through a dam can allow the rancher to balance the flow so that beavers have plenty of water, and flooding is minimized. Ranchers with beaver streams have been able to assist their neighbors who find themselves caught in cycles of drought. In mountain meadows, naturalists practice beaver biomimicry to retain water and to sift out ash and sediment from fire debris. There is so much to learn from these wise waterkeepers.[20]

Benyus brings an arguably ground-shifting perspective to our conversation about becoming edge species. Doubtless we are aware, at least in general terms, of Charles Darwin's theory of *survival of the fittest*. Benyus tells us that Darwin did not use the term *fittest* originally. In the first four editions of *On the Origin of Species*, he wrote about survival of the *fit*. And that word difference changes everything. She explains that organisms seek to *fit* to a place, to a community. They don't simply move to a location; they help cocreate a place, and, forever changing, it creates them.[21]

Wow! There it is. What is mine to do when I no longer fit within a community because the community is changing? How do I evolve my behaviors to become more at home where I am? How do I help the helpers when lives are changing? I find it touching that Beynus speaks of coming back to fitness as a *homecoming*. Surely, we can begin a list of what must change for us to fit to place, to help the helpers. What about addressing our hubris, lack of curiosity, penchant for managing instead of helping, inability to listen, ignoring the genius of kith and kin? What will you add to this list? This is our pilgrimage: becoming fit to the living world around us, coming home to our truest selves, reweaving frayed connections.

■ ■ ■

I wander the nearby woods, noticing my attraction to fixing things. I pray to humble myself so that I might acknowledge the genius of tree and plant teachers and learn from them. Listen with my senses, heart, and soul. Imagine that I might become sufficiently permeable to receive what may be offered. Honor the possibility of soul-to-soul communion. I remind myself that every living being has evolved with its own intelligence, propensity for life, and a multitude of connections to others. Not one lifeform has ever been found to be independent. How will I adapt to fit this place? What helpers might I help?

What place is calling you? Visit often. Don't talk—or even think in words. Stay in the present moment, available to the life around you. Move slowly in the space, trying not to disturb the network of beings who are there. Linger. Stand, sit, lie down. Gaze into the distance; then close in. Take in the grand and the microscopic. What plants or insects seem to support or perhaps harm each other? Hold assumptions lightly, noticing without forming rigid conclusions. Imagine the connections that are occurring underground and above you. What patterns are making themselves known, suggesting the unseen? Wordlessly ask of the trees or the stream or the birds, "What do you want me to know? What support do you need?"

If we are to become capable of adapting and supporting mutual thriving now and well into the future, we must cocreate with the living world around us. There is no going it alone. Blessedly, we are traveling in the company of geniuses.

NINE

On the Threshold

◼

Place and mind may interpenetrate
till the nature of both is altered.[1]

NAN SHEPHERD

Threshold (*noun):* the sill of a doorway; the
entrance to a house or building; any place or point
of entering or beginning, as in *the threshold of a new
career.* Also called *limen (psychology, physiology),*
the point at which a stimulus is of sufficient
intensity to begin to produce an effect, as in *the
threshold of consciousness; a low threshold of pain.*[2]

Humanity stands at the threshold, a doorway
between endings and beginnings. There is no turning back. The epoch of the Holocene, which began 11,700
years ago and has been so supportive of life, is succumbing to the sixth mass extinction known to Earth. Previous
extinctions happened over thousands of years; the one we
are living now is predicted to take only decades more. Our
planetary home will continue to see the loss of fragile and
important ecosystems, disruption of food webs and water
cycles, and significant impacts on our way of life. Some of

us may have sufficient resources to allow us to continue for a few more years under the illusion that we can maintain our lifestyle. Yet, the longer we take to change course, the more intense and extensive the loss of life. If we continue to ignore the limits of growth, shun our connections with all beings, deny our place in the cosmos, and resist changing how we live, we will ensure even greater catastrophic loss.

This requires deep listening and discernment of the next steps, even as the edges crumble around us and we long for a ready solution. But perhaps there are no solutions. Perhaps we are facing profound *predicaments* rather than *problems*. ". . . [A] *problem* calls for a solution; the only question is whether one can be found and made to work, and once this is done, the problem is solved. A *predicament*, by contrast, has no solution. Faced with a predicament, people come up with responses."[3] Regardless of how successful any response might be, it cannot eliminate the predicament.

The melting of glaciers. The rapid decline of birds and insects. The demise of vast stretches of oceanic ecosystems. Nearly ubiquitous plastic. Amid a multitude of predicaments, we have an opportunity to step over the threshold into new ways of living in which we honor, care for, and collaborate with kith and kin, as we align with the dream of Earth and cosmos. Our rational mind will offer some contributions, but it does not belong in the driver's seat as we face predicaments. If we depend only upon previous experiences and logic to guide our next steps, we are likely to create just another iteration of business as usual that will be woefully insufficient for our collective future. Without cultivating new perspectives, we may think, for instance, that we can count on political leaders to sanction a fail-safe technology to reduce carbon or that wealthy businessmen will take us to a new home on another planet if we ruin this one.

We will depend upon dreamers, storytellers, soul connectors, and heart weavers to guide us in collectively reimagining how to live in full kinship as Earth's richly diverse family. There is no healthy way forward that prioritizes the needs of some of us over those of others, for we exist only in relationships. We have spent lifetimes picking away at the threads that bind us, and we see the disaster in progress that was born of a life with only fragile ties to kith and kin. We do not fully understand how to proceed toward universal thriving, but proceed together we must, inspired by a dream that is still taking shape.

The roles of navigator and captain on this journey belong to heart and soul. Only when we rely upon and collaborate with wisdom greater than our own will we be able to respond in life-giving ways to the predicaments our world is facing. As we wrestle with complex, life-defining questions, we must listen for wisdom embedded within us and throughout the cosmos, allowing it to flow through us and guide our actions.

■ ■ ■

On the threshold. Seek the place from which you've come? Step into the unknown? Linger for a time? How does one decide?

For several years, I've collaborated with colleagues to lead retreats that align with the February 1 feast day of St. Brigid of Kildare. Patron Saint of Ireland, Brigid lived from 451 to 525 and founded an abbey at Kildare, a double monastery that included both women and men. Although much of her story has been lost in the mists of time, it is said that her mother was a Christian Pict slave and her father, a Druid Irish chieftain. Is it any wonder that we associate Brigid with thresholds, standing as she did at the doorway between slave and free, Christian and Druid, rich and poor, the powerful and powerless, feminine and masculine? Living in edge times, on the threshold, Brigid was known for her hospitality and her stand for equality. She was a woman of influence in whose story we can find inspiration and wisdom for today.

Legend has it that Brigid was born at the threshold of her mother's home. While that may be apocryphal, history tells us that expectant mothers of that time often stood at the doorway of their small cottages, pushing against the frame until their child was delivered. Sometimes they were aided by a *kneeling woman*, the midwife who would wait on her knees on the hard-packed floor to assist in the birth.

Brigid's story and that of countless women of the past remind us of vital considerations as we stand at the threshold: What is waiting to be born in us? What are we being called to midwife? These are urgent questions to which heart and soul are now called. Even if the answers ultimately prove to be beyond our complete understanding, the questions are deeply worthy of our struggle, and we will gain strength by wrestling with them.

■ ■ ■

What is waiting to be born in you? Pause to absorb the depth of this question. This is not a conversation about adding solar panels, replanting trees, or writing petitions; it begs us to consider how we might live fully alive in our truest, deepest self. We must descend to our pre-rational soul, to the deep, sacred mystery beyond our understanding, and allow it to transform and guide us.

Embracing the dream of Earth will require deep listening. To move into the future will require that we sink back "'into the source of everything,' during which we must learn to trust our unknowing...."[4] Stepping across the threshold will require leaving much behind. It is time for death and resurrection.

Let's return to the story that takes place in a dark cave where an old woman is weaving the tapestry of the world. Boldly, I place myself in that story, wondering if I might be granted the dream of a new and more beautiful design. I am haunted by the black dog and ponder why he tears at the weaving. What is his role in death and rebirth? I think of our own dogs and the incredible sense of smell they possess. I wonder, could it be that, guided by scent, the dog is seizing upon threads that are rotting? Perhaps he is snagging threads of separation, competition, egotism, and othering, threads that, to my chagrin, I have too often woven into the tapestry of my life. Could it be possible that the black dog is assisting the realization of the dream by dragging away threads that do not offer vitality and hope? If I, if we, can acknowledge threads that do not sustain mutual thriving, might we eliminate them and so weave a more just, compassionate, and beautiful world?

■ ■ ■

It's easy to talk or write about leaving our old ways behind, but living that way is difficult. It was about ten years ago. The tree towered over the second story window, its leaves nearly touching the screen just beyond where I sat. In the old farmhouse, air conditioning was limited to window units, and I valued both the beauty of the tree and the protection it offered from the afternoon sun. For quite some time I had resisted my husband's recommendation to cut her down. I loved the closeness I felt to the treetops and the birds singing in her purple-flowered branches, their scent wafting on the gentle breeze.

It took only a bit of research to yield her guilty secret: she was an Empress Tree, a fast-growing invasive. She had begun dropping her branches over the past few seasons, and the large holes in her trunk suggested that she was hollow. Given the strong winds that sometimes shook our hilltop home, it was becoming increasingly likely that she might fall on our house during a storm. I resigned myself to the fact that cutting her down was the logical thing to do.

The day arrived when she was to be taken down. The upper branches were lassoed, severed from their source, and lowered into the yard. Untethered leaves and flowers took to the air and wafted to the ground. Then the saws were turned on the trunk. Several feet in diameter, she was cut down in sections, revealing her hollow core where heartwood should have been. The noise increased as each section grew larger until the work came to a halt at the ground and the crew turned to digging up the stump and roots. Across the yard lay scattered sections of what had once been a living tree.

The din had dulled, and the cleanup was underway when I noticed movement in the raised bed of my nearby herb garden. Assuming a rabbit had arrived in search of a tasty meal, I leaned toward the bed and clapped my hands. Out of the herbs ran a small squirrel. With a look of utter panic, he ran across the yard to where the tree had been, stopped dead, and then ran back to the herb garden seeking cover. In an instant I saw the world through his eyes: his home destroyed, separated from his family, a trembling roar and his world ended.

I left large sections of trunk in the yard, hoping that the squirrel family might return, but of course those meager sections were a poor substitute for the once-tall tree. My efforts were too little, too late. It didn't matter that I hadn't realized that a family inhabited the tree. I had made the decision without giving it a thought.

The decision to cut down the tree was logical and rational. It made sense. I have spent most of my life making decisions by drawing on logic and rational thought. Like many, I have been rewarded for listening and responding from my thinking mind: look back at previous experiences, analyze the situation, consider the pros and cons of possible actions, and make a decision. *A windstorm could topple the tree onto our house, and, after all, the species is invasive.*

But there is another way of making decisions that begins with listening from our heart wisdom, *mind-in-heart* as the mystics would say, open and present to greater Wisdom within us and all beings of the cosmos. In the attitude of mind-in-heart, wisdom flows from an incomprehensible source that we might call Spirit or Mystery. It is in this space that we may hear ourselves saying things we didn't know we knew. Or we might sense a wordless understanding that is impossible to explain. I *feel* your fear. I *sense* other choices that might be invited.

Of course, for many day-to-day decisions, experience and a bit of logic may be just what's needed. The decision to switch to a new brand of toothpaste comes to mind as one silly but simple example. But decisions that impact others are often ill-served by the approach that most of us learned to weigh decisions. You've probably made lists of the pros and cons of one choice over another, and so you know that it doesn't always work. Perhaps you've set out a list of reasons to leave your job and another list to suggest why you should stay. Then you stare helplessly as you see that despite the length of one list or the weight of one item over another, you still feel unsure and confused. That's because whether to leave your job is usually a decision that belongs to the heart, not the logic of the mind. What's invited is *discernment*.

■ ■ ■

The term is familiar, but what does *discernment* really mean? Underlying the practice of discernment is the assumption that wisdom, spirit, God, love—the name or no-name that you use for the deep mystery that is more than we can comprehend—is at work within and around each of us and throughout the universe. In discernment, we do our best to silence our busy minds that are trying to figure out what we're called to do, and rest in the quiet of our hearts to listen for the still, small voice that invites our next step. We sift through the voices of ego, friends, or popular culture that are urging a particular action until we are able to distinguish the voice of Wisdom, who often reveals herself through nudges, whispers, feelings, or sensory experiences.

We are told that God spoke directly to Moses through a burning bush. I don't know of anyone else who's had that specific experience, and personally I'm not expecting anything of the sort. But I do know that wisdom speaks to me through bushes—and roses, sparrows, thunder, rivers, and many other dimensions of the living world. A moment of clarity arises on the wind. Trees whisper a word. A dragonfly causes me to pause and offers a reminder. And that seems to be true for many people. The sacred is incarnate in nature, even as wisdom is beyond all we know and see. So, it's not surprising that many people say that they feel closer to a holy presence when they are in the forest, along the coast, or gazing at the stars.

Discernment often begins with a wondering, a question that may be articulated or perhaps remains fuzzy and unformed. I've learned to hold this beginning stage lightly, because it often turns out that the question I think is important is not the one I most need to explore. So that first sense of direction that comes to me is, at best, a possibility. The challenge is to stay in a space of wondering, noticing, watching, and waiting. I want to be open, present, aware. Silencing my busy thoughts is important; it clears a space for what is to come. But what works for me might not be ideal for you. You too might choose to sit in silence, or perhaps you will want to dance under the stars. You may find support from a clearness committee, a Quaker practice where a group of people commit to listening together for the answer that lies within you. Whatever brings you closer to heart and soul and further from the hamster wheel of figuring out the answer is what's invited.

Be aware that the way a question starts to sharpen, or an answer begins to form is unpredictable and may take you by surprise. You may receive just the nudge or word that was needed from a friend, a stranger, a poem, or a sunset. Sometimes an experience of awe and wonder offers the clarity you need, perhaps when you were unaware that you were longing for it.

Discernment isn't a process that responds to our schedule even though we are often impatient for an answer. Our thinking, planning minds can find it difficult to wait for the next step to be revealed. And to add to our frustration, we sometimes find that it is only the next step that is shown to us. Or perhaps we have a sense of the things we are called to do, but no understanding of why. When we're invited on a journey, we want to understand the destination and why it's important to travel there. It's difficult to fathom that we might be called to add one piece to a puzzle that will not be completed or perhaps even take shape in our lifetime.

I once read about a wise prophet who was in conversation with a small group of volunteers. These good people wanted to know what the prophet thought about the positive action they'd taken. The sage replied, "I think this is very good. There will likely be excellent results from this in about six hundred years."

■ ■ ■

The fog rolls in softly, creeping over the hills and creating new folds of landscape as colors fade to black and white. No longer able clearly to see the road ahead, I slow my car. With sounds muffled, I relish the shifting configuration of low clouds, the new shapes of once familiar objects, and the quiet solitude of my journey. The fog intensifies, and I slow again. A term from a long-ago driver's manual comes to mind: *overdriving your headlights*. Overdriving your headlights occurs when you go so fast that your stopping distance is farther than the illuminated area of your headlights. The manual warns of the danger of crashing into an object ahead. Indeed! I note with chagrin this fitting description of how I act all too often.

When I am blessed with a sliver of wisdom, and I can see just the next step I'm invited to take, I often have a moment of gratitude. Then curiosity (or could it be a need for control?) takes over; I want to know more. Where am I going? I could get there so much better/faster/more efficiently if I knew where *there* was. Indulging my thinking mind, I hypothesize the outcome: ah, that must be what I am called to do! Then, confident of my knowledge (there goes the thinking mind again!), I leap into action, running pell-mell ahead of what I've been given to do, or, as a friend says, "I'm running ahead of grace."

What is it within us that seeks to outwit the fog of this life? Can we not slow our speed, enjoy the shifting shapes present in the moment, rest in the softness and quiet of this part of the journey, and trust that the path ahead will be illuminated in its time? Our logical, rational mind is so helpful in many situations; it can be a great partner in implementing the actions that we've discerned. Yet our mind can be undisciplined, unwilling to accept the limitations of our knowledge, uncomfortable without seeing the whole plan, annoyed at the inefficiency and slowness of traveling without a clear destination. Given the complexity of the predicaments we face in these edge times, our way will not be all sunshine and roses. We will have many opportunities to drive in the fog. We will need to practice simply discerning the next step, and then the next step, and then the next, trusting the wisdom we are given without knowing the future or the results of our efforts.

■ ■ ■

As we stand at the threshold, we realize that discerning our next step must not rely on our understanding alone.

If we could engage soul to soul with the natural world, we might glimpse Earth's dream and our role in helping to manifest it. As you dive into your soul journey, other souls who are also dreaming of a world in which all beings thrive may make themselves known to you. After all, you are kindred spirits on this path. And sometimes it helps to have a practice that encourages you to connect more deeply with the natural world. I invite you to a practice of *pilgrimaging close to home.*[5]

You are probably aware of some of the pilgrimage sites of various religious traditions, such as Mecca, the Holy Land, the island of Iona off the coast of Scotland, or Santiago de Compostela. The rich tradition of pilgrimages goes back centuries and includes travel to holy sites of ancient groves, sacred waters, mountains, deserts, remarkable landscapes, or sacred structures created by early peoples. But as profound as such pilgrimage experiences can be, you don't need to travel long distances or follow ancient traditions to experience deep connection. The holy space of creation is all around us, and the heart of the pilgrim is always within us. Join me in such a pilgrimage. Set aside several hours, or even half a day, if possible, for the first portion of our pilgrimage, and let's travel with a pilgrim heart.

Identify a place near you where, to the extent possible, you may wander with a variety of species. Forested areas are often ecologically rich and diverse. Or perhaps you'll want to choose a location where there are edges, where water and land, trees and pasture, marsh and dry land meet. If you live in a city, consider a wooded park, nature preserve, botanical garden, river, or even a community garden. This practice may be easier for you if the sounds of people and machines are not prominent, but if you lack that level of quiet, don't let it dissuade you from the practice. Your experience may be rich if you connect with your pilgrim heart to even a single tree. A short distance with terrain that does not challenge your physical ability is perfect. Think of this as a saunter with frequent stops or a time to sit quietly.

Pack light. Leave behind social media. Perhaps even leave your phone behind. Leave anything that might weigh you down, including expectations, concerns, plans, and lists. You might build a small stone cairn near the beginning of your walk with each stone representing something you are choosing not to carry on this journey. The cairn is a reminder that your concern or worry will still be there upon your return if you choose to retrieve it. Carry only what you need, such as a water bottle and perhaps a blanket to sit on. Dress for variable weather so that you will not be distracted by physical discomfort. (NOTE: This guidance assumes that your close-to-home pilgrimage is in an area where the terrain and surroundings are safe. If you're unsure, take whatever you need for safety's sake, pilgrimage with a partner, and let someone know where you are going and when you're expecting to return.)

Set an intention for deeper connection. Place your hands over your heart, and invite your pilgrim heart to stay open, present, and connected to what is, just as it is. Begin by walking slowly, perhaps without a clear destination. Name your desire for deeper connections to this place. Hold anything more specific than that as lightly as a butterfly perched on your shoulder, enjoying what it has to offer and knowing that at any time it may fly off to be replaced by what you truly need but didn't know it.

Tune your five-stringed harp. One by one, focus on each of your senses and allow them to sharpen. (There is more detail about this in Chapter 5 if you need a reminder.)

Spend time with kith and kin. Choose a companion from the natural world—or let a companion choose you. Perhaps you feel drawn to be with a portion of the land or a plant, animal, or insect. Make yourself comfortable standing, sitting, or lying down as near to your companion as possible. Gaze. Stay attentive. Be present. This may be difficult, especially for the first ten or fifteen minutes, as your mind will wander and want to claim your attention. A little voice may suggest that this is a waste of time, that you have better things to do. Acknowledge that your mind is busy, and then return to this place, this time, this/these kith and kin. Attend. Notice. Simply be open, present, and connected.

Offer your gratitude. At some point it will be time to leave. But before you say good-bye to the kin with whom you've been spending time, offer your gratitude. Touch into your heart and allow gratefulness for this being to well up within you. If it feels right, name it aloud.

Bring home the blessing. Don't let it fade. Nurture the gifts of this time in your heart. Write about it in your journal. Reflect on what you've noticed.

Return often. At some point, after your soul friendship deepens, you may silently ask your companion what they know of the dream of Earth. Or perhaps ask what they would like for you to know.

Variations. You need not make the pilgrimage alone; walk with friends or family if you choose. You'll probably want to agree to some guidelines before setting out to ensure that you are not expected to keep up a friendly chit-chat that pulls you away from being present. If you have small children and cannot find time to go on a pilgrimage alone, take them. Open to seeing the world through their eyes. Invite them to point out to you what they hear, see, smell. Lie on a blanket together and watch the clouds or the squirrels in the trees. You can learn about being present to nature from a child.

* * *

As we stand on this threshold, we see that time and again we've made the decision to choose self over kindom. Here in this doorway, we see that the beautiful, flawed, awe-inspiring, and sorrow-filled world we have loved both well and poorly cannot last if we continue as we have been. We have sacrificed the lives and homes of those least like us so that those most like us could continue our unsustainable way of life for as long as possible. We have ignored the basic needs of the next generation for the comfort of our current lifestyle. The web of life has been battered. Lost from our truest selves, we have frayed the threads that bind us to kith and kin.

Out of the chaos of the great flaring forth this universe formed. On the edges of converging ecosystems, ecotones enable species to evolve and flourish. The past need not predict the future. The call rings forth: imagine a new future in collaboration with Earth's wisdom, reweave communion with kith and kin, return to the universal tree of life and liveliness. You have a unique purpose in these uncertain times; the critical work of discerning your soul's mission rests with you. Here on this threshold, tend to what is being born in your soul.

TEN

Leadership for Edge Times

*We must die to our old way of belonging to
the world to enable us to uncover something
radical, something new, something we could
never have rationally deduced, something that
our individual and collective lives depended on.*[1]

BILL PLOTKIN

The reverberations of the singing bowl are the only
sound in the room. We sit in silence, our chairs
encircling a small table where a candle is burning. This
is the beginning of our weekly staff meeting. The silence
continues and deepens for me as I gradually slow and
then release the thoughts that come unbidden. In this
contemplative prayer time, the focus is on listening
from the spiritual heart. Open, present, available to the
whispers and nudging of the spirit—the Great Mystery,
Wisdom, Love—who, regardless of the name we use, we

believe is actively at work throughout the cosmos and in our lives.

After a half hour of silence, the leader for that morning again invites the bell, and we listen silently until the last audible vibration fades away. The bell serves as a reminder of the importance of listening deeply. Anyone may invite the bell at any time during the business meeting that is to follow if the conversation feels too "heady" or if the person senses that we just need time to pause and sink into our hearts. I notice the physical changes that happen for me in the minute or so of silence after the bell. Shoulders drop, my breath deepens, my mind relaxes, and I reenter the conversation from a different place, as do others.

I stepped into this tradition of weekly staff meetings from 2009 to 2015 when I served as the executive director of the Shalem Institute for Spiritual Formation in Washington, D.C., a nonprofit dedicated to supporting contemplative living and leadership. Meetings of the board of directors and committees also began with this practice of listening, a tradition that had become deeply ingrained in the charism of the organization from its inception forty years prior. Although it might appear that the point of this practice was silence, the intention was listening. Our hope was that the practice of being fully present would weave its way into our lives and work, opening us to ongoing discernment.

In many ways, our office was like that of other small nonprofits. We enjoyed conversations over morning coffee and laughed often as we sat together at lunchtime. We raised funds, managed budgets, prepared for the multiple programs we offered, put out regular newsletters, updated social media, and answered phones and emails. Yet undergirding all these activities was a different understanding of leadership.

■ ■ ■

Over the three decades prior to working at Shalem, my work had revolved around leadership. I served in leadership roles in large corporations, taught courses to managers, consulted on leadership issues, and coached hundreds of senior executives. I rode the waves of trends, theories, and research, read volumes, and participated in conferences both as a learner and as an expert. I wrote countless articles and blogs, and designed or reviewed more management courses than I can recall. Let me distill these 60,000+ hours of practice into a single sentence that reflects what I've learned: The models of leadership that I have seen most often promoted and practiced are ill-suited for the world in which we are living and are quite likely harmful to our collective future.

It took many years for me to realize that what I had considered to be well-honed wisdom was not serving the needs of leaders or these uncertain times. When the shaky framework on which I had built much of my career became apparent, I began searching for another way of leading. Even though I had no practical experience in it, I knew enough about *contemplative leadership* to be drawn to its potential. I had participated in programs offered by Shalem, so when I was invited to lead the organization, I hoped that I could both lead and learn. My six years there turned out to be one of the formative experiences of my life.

I came to appreciate that contemplative leadership is not another iteration of popular models; it is a fundamental reframing of what it means to be a leader. Contemplative leadership is grounded in the stream of Holy Mystery at work in the world, leading toward a dream of justice, compassion, and wholeness. It understands that our hearts have been endowed with wisdom and compassion and that spirit is ever at work in our lives.

Before we proceed, I want to make clear that you do not have to work at Shalem to embrace contemplative leadership. You do not need to work in an organization that focuses on spirituality. In fact, you do not need to work in any organization to practice contemplative leadership. If you are hoping to save a nearby forest, trying to bring your community together to address a particular need, or wondering how to live more fully into your soul's calling, you are called to leadership, and this is relevant.

As I have done throughout this book, I offer my experiences in hopes that they might suggest possibilities for you, in this case possibilities that will take us all beyond traditional leadership models that I believe have serious limitations.

Many models assume a single leader or a few individuals in designated roles who draw on their extensive knowledge and experience to establish a vision, motivate followers, and solve problems so that the organization can accomplish certain predetermined goals. If the goals are incremental and short term and the challenges are both narrow in scope and similar to past issues, such leadership may serve. But we need a more robust approach to leadership in these edge times. Here's why.

First, we are facing predicaments that typical approaches cannot adequately address. For example, who can clearly envision a solution to the drying up of the Colorado River? After two decades of drought, the nation's largest reservoirs are nearly three-quarters empty, and the seven states and thirty tribes that rely on the river for drinking water, irrigation, and electrical power struggle to agree on how to address this crisis. Many of our current issues are *unsolvable*, complex, overlapping, and existential. There is no clear answer that will set everything right. We face systemic issues with many interwoven values and the lives of millions depend upon our action or inaction.

Second, because lifestyles, livelihoods, and lives are often at stake, emotions will run high. Even superb application of a logical, rational approach will not necessarily align minds, hearts, and souls. We will have to find a deeper common thread of love and mutuality if we are to move forward with a common purpose. Much of the work that needs to be done is beyond changing processes or structures; we ourselves must change. Leadership for this time requires great compassion for and commitment to others and deep soul-searching for ourselves.

Third, because we have never faced predicaments on such a scale, leadership cannot evolve from an individual effort but must arise from collaboration. No individual can count on their personal knowledge and experience to be sufficient for the task. We must draw on the collective wisdom of people from diverse backgrounds and beliefs as well as the wisdom of our wider kith and kin. The more diverse and inclusive the process, the greater the likelihood of finding a way forward together.

This leads us to the fourth premise that I heard first from my spiritual mentor: Everyone is a leader at the point of their gifts. Everyone's leadership is needed. I'm not suggesting that everyone is leading in every moment and on every issue but that everyone is called to leadership in fulfillment of their soul's mission. There is no room for any of us to deumur or hide behind perceived inadequacies. We are invited to trust that when we have faithfully discerned what work is ours to do in this time, we will be given the capacity for leadership. For the sake of the world, we each must step into the role as leader in alignment with our soul's call. We trust that steps we need to take will be shown to us as we deepen our sense of purpose and align with the dream of the universe. Indeed, the future is already unfolding around us; we can glimpse it with the eyes of the heart. Contemplative leadership is a response to our communion with and love for the world and the unique mission to which spirit calls us.

■ ■ ■

From where does the leader derive power? In most traditional leadership models, we consider that power flows from one's position or title. Sometimes, because of an individual's expertise, competence, education, confidence, or even bravado, people choose to follow them. Sometimes leaders emerge because they can offer rewards or punishment and accepting their directives seems to be in the best interest of the followers. It is generally accepted that to be a leader, I have more of "it" than others have, or I have been given authority or control for a particular purpose. Such power is far too limiting for the work of reclaiming our place in this family of life.

If we consider power as *the capacity to act in alignment with the invitation of the universe*, then we must begin by accepting our soul's calling that will guide us to transformative action. We cannot reimagine ourselves from our current worldviews; we cannot *rationally* reinvent ourselves. We must connect to and be transformed by mystery beyond our knowing. The source of power is always flowing from Spirit, whose very breath gives life to the dream of the universe. In her book *Discernment*, Rose

Mary Dougherty noted that discernment is not just for special occasions. Rather it is a daily practice, an ongoing way of being, a gift available to each of us.[2] As contemplative leaders, we live in ongoing discernment as we seek to align with the unfolding work of the spirit.

We are called to listen deeply to our heart's wisdom, to those with whom we are living and working, to the kith and kin in our locale and beyond, and to Earth. This stance of deep listening opens us to a stream of wisdom that feeds our work, helping us to align with what is waiting to be born and what is ours to midwife. This collective intelligence is a gift from the family of beings, and it connects us to the emerging future.

■ ■ ■

At the heart of contemplative leadership is *communion*, a wordless sharing or exchange of feelings and thoughts as one being. Our hearts are born to entrain with other hearts, our souls with other souls. We feel sad when others cry; we pick up anxiety from those around us. We respond with smiles to the joyful giggles of children and are often drawn to chuckle at the genuine, can't-stop laughter of people we don't even know. It may seem strange to speak of sharing feelings without words, but when we stop to consider, we see that it happens often. And this is true of our relationship with the more-than-human world too.

When we fenced the cattle out of the stream at our farm, it never occurred to us that the deer who crossed nightly from field to forest might find the fence an insurmountable obstacle. And most of the herd jumped the fence without a moment's pause. Yet there I stood one crisp evening watching helplessly as the herd cleared the fence and left behind a fawn too insecure to make the leap. As he ran up and down the fence line in search of a way forward, my heart hurt for his confusion and fear. Communion is more than empathy, though it includes that. It's a recognition of oneness, of the unbroken ties of the web of life, an acknowledgement that everything is woven together and there is no "other."

Inherent in communion is the gift of *compassion*. This bears further discussion as compassion is all too often thought to interfere with leadership. There was a time I would have stopped reading at this point, saturated as I was in the belief that leaders should adhere to policies and procedures and follow them with few exceptions. A manager must never wear her heart on her sleeve. When I assumed a leadership role in Human Resources (HR) in a well-known corporation, I discovered an inside joke that went like this: "Someone told me that they wanted to work in HR because they liked people!" Cue the laughter of those on the inside. Ha. Ha. I laughed along at the irony of it and thought it must be true.

In my experience, the best approach for the few female executives who had hopes of climbing the corporate ladder was to follow in the footsteps of our male counterparts. That began with dressing the part: pin-striped suit; starched shirt of a muted, solid color or stripes, small scarf tied into a bow. It continued with acting the part: firm, confident, no nonsense, keep to the rules. Whether setting policy or making decisions, one always began with logic and reason. It was okay to check in with your feelings after that if you didn't get carried away by them. That approach seemed to work well, supporting my upward climb to more responsibility, more staff, and higher compensation. At least it worked well until I found, like many of my colleagues, that it wasn't enough. I had a job that many would envy, and my soul was parched.

For a while, I tried to feed my heart and soul on the side as I continued to serve the company and hold a position I valued. It took two years of deliberation before I was able to wrench myself from the corner office, the parking space, the title, the money, a sense of accomplishment, and yes, the power and status. My deepest fear was that without the title I would not know who I was. Corporations perpetuate the myth of the executive's importance; it keeps the machine alive.

Yet, compassionate leadership can still break through in corporations. One example has stayed with me, perhaps because it was so countercultural. I was working as an executive coach in a large organization with a senior executive whom I'll call John. The environment was fast-paced, results-oriented, and bottom-line focused—a typical corporation, in other words. During one of our coaching sessions, John shared with me what he had discovered while participating in a leadership training program.

During one part of the program, participants were divided into pairs for role plays that were videotaped. John was assigned to play the role of the boss; his colleague played the role of John's employee who wanted to gain approval for a new project. As the employee tried to interest John in a new idea, John pretended to be distracted by his email. He had to respond to "just this one message." A few minutes later, John's phone rang, and he interrupted his colleague to "take this important call." As the camera recorded their exchange, John's "employee" continued to try to get the attention of a distracted, multitasking John.

At the conclusion of the role play, John and his colleague watched the video together. The stated intention of the training session had been to learn to influence more effectively those in authority. John told me that he learned something entirely different from watching the video. He saw his colleague—a smart, competent, normally poised individual—become flustered and upset because of John's apparent disregard for him. Immediately, John felt compassion for this individual who was trying so hard to be seen and heard.

Even more troubling to John was the realization that his behavior as the boss during the role play, while somewhat exaggerated, wasn't all that different from his day-to-day behavior. He saw how those who worked for him could feel disrespected and demeaned. As he watched the video play back, John was not thinking about productivity or efficiency; he was seeing with the eyes of his heart.

In that moment, John set an intention to be more fully present in day-to-day conversations with his team. This wasn't an easy commitment on which to follow through. Especially in the beginning weeks, he felt the tug of "things to do" and the longing to try to multitask. Yet as he practiced his intention, it became easier. He began to count on the knowledge and experience of the entire team as they built the trust and respect needed to share more fully with John—who was now listening.

The compassion John felt for his colleague in that simple role play opened the possibility for interacting differently with others. We all have been gifted with compassion. And scientists confirm what many of us have intuitively known: we are hard-wired for compassion. At times we may struggle against it, but it is always there, available to us within the deep wisdom of the heart. When we listen and respond only from our ego, we think only of our own concerns. When we listen and respond only from our rational mind, we consider primarily what we can do to change the situation. When we listen with our "mind in heart," we allow space for deeper wisdom to emerge.

■ ■ ■

Surely, we have responsibility for the bold, personal journey to the depths of our soul and for forming deep connections to our kin. Yet moving toward the evolving future will require many unified efforts. Our leadership must be *collaborative*. The world needs the engagement and involvement of people of diverse backgrounds, experiences, and beliefs who can collaborate in the recommitment of our lives for the well-being of all. We need guidance from those who have practiced openness to the teachings of Earth and all beings. As we have discussed, many Indigenous peoples have long embraced kincentric ecology, developing over generations an understanding of the needs of the living world and listening to her wisdom. What a gift it is for others of us to learn from those who have schooled themselves in the wisdom of kith and kin!

We must remember that we are not expected to figure out how to address complex predicaments. Our role is to listen deeply and then allow what is being invited to emerge within and through us. And even when we have a sense of what might be invited, it is important to hold it lightly and continue to discern the rightness of our steps. Although we may sense a strong call to move in a particular direction, the destination, as we've noted before, will not always be clear. It's all too easy to run ahead of grace, to sense that we know everything because the first few steps seem apparent to us. Discernment is a lifelong practice. We must forever return to the voice of Wisdom, that voice that guides our next steps. I am not suggesting that there is nothing else we must do, but rather what is ours to do must flow from the essence of our truest self as we are guided by the sacred mystery.

Perhaps one of our most important acts of leadership may be to create the space for soul work for ourselves and others. We can sit at the feet of Indigenous and people of color to listen to their stories and receive their wisdom as they feel it is right for them to share. We can engage and embrace the experiences of younger adults and follow their lead while offering support and encouragement. We can learn to know deeply the land around us, acknowledge her rhythms, and learn to live in communion with kin we have neglected for too long.

■ ■ ■

Creativity is inherent in the design of the cosmos, the immense spiraling creation formed from the great flaring forth: the birthing of stars and supernovas, the symmetry of solar systems, the miracle of expanding vastness. Earth, the uniquely exquisite daughter of the universe, has been birthing from her beginning: separating water and land; begetting single cells that divide and multiply; creating flourishing, flowering beauty that gifts the planet with color, sound, and movement; rebirthing after devastating earthquakes, volcanoes, fires, floods—and even great extinction events. As far as we can understand, Earth leans toward diversity and abundance. She is ever creating, life bringing forth life.

We are the products of stars with generations of creativity embedded in our DNA, children of an ever-creating universe. For ancient peoples, the world around them was a source of imagination and creativity. So it can be for us. As Matthew Fox wrote, "[W]e generate in communion with the Divine who dwells *and* generates within us."[3]

Throughout this book, we have discussed the weaving of awe and wonder with that of grief and sorrow. It is the often-chaotic interactions of these soul-journey paths that open us to more vibrant creativity and transformation. Where ecosystems collide, an ecotone emerges to offer a habitat that contains elements of both its parents and yet is unique unto itself. In the darkness, new seeds can be birthed, bringing forth heretofore unimagined liveliness. Out of the chaos of a weaving destroyed, a new and more beautiful design may emerge. From our collective impasse, a new way may be given. This is the generative possibility that leaders in edge times are called to embrace: we are called to a pilgrimage along the cliff edge to a place we cannot imagine on a path not yet forged as we discern each step together.

There is good news. This is not ours to do alone. Earth herself has been creating and recreating for four and a half billion years. True, we have damaged or destroyed some of her more diverse, beautiful, and life-giving creations. It's past time to own up to how we have harmed Earth, past time to humbly work to make amends. But we should be clear that Earth has agency. It is not ours to do *to* or *for* Earth. That has not worked well in the past. Although it may have taken hundreds of millions of years, Earth has recovered from great disasters and will do so again. It is ours to collaborate with her for the sake of the lives that yet may be saved.

Each of us is invited to leadership in these edge times for the sake of the evolving future. What is required of us has been shaped by the very essence of who we are. It is time to step courageously out of the old ways that center on individual knowledge and needs. It is time for radical trust in the sacred call to mutual care and flourishing. It has been given to us to plant the trees that will mature in future lifetimes. We are called to lay steppingstones for others to follow. We must pick up the threads and begin reweaving the great and beautiful tapestry of soul and Earth, for we are the ancestors of the future.

ELEVEN

Choosing Stories for the Future

*The end of the world as we know it is not the end of
the world, full stop. . . . (W)e live within stories whose
ending lies beyond the horizon of our lifetimes.*[1]

DOUGALD HINE

I remember a skirt perfect for swirling and spinning,
made from three lengths of pink floral cotton, sewn
by my mother on the shiny black machine with "SINGER"
inscribed in bold gold letters accompanied by flourishes.
It had two rounds of basting threads, just a few centime-
ters apart, stitched around the top. She left the threads
long to wrap around her fingers so she could pull the
gathers to fit the waist of her just-turned-six-year-old. As
she worked the fine stitches of the hem, was she hopeful
for me, her only daughter? Did it make her sad to send

me off to school for the first time and alter the household rhythm? Or perhaps it would be a relief to focus only on my brother during the day.

Crinolines under the skirt added volume and flounce. Blond hair pulled back tightly into a ponytail, bangs newly trimmed. Short, of course. I could turn and turn and turn in this amazing skirt and never stop, such was the exhilaration of spinning in a circle of petticoats.

Hand in my mother's hand, I walk through the double doors and up the steps of the red brick building that houses our small country school. She leaves me at the door of a classroom, the one for grades one to four. Seven first graders are assigned to the wooden desks in the front row, nearest the teacher. Although Mrs. Caldwell has teen-age daughters of her own, it's her first year as well. What does she see in these scrubbed faces, in the eyes that follow her expectantly? The room is a cauldron of possibility. Hope dances with fear and doubt.

Three recesses: mid-morning, after lunch, and mid-afternoon. We are usually left without adult supervision to play on the swings and slide or devise our own entertainment. It doesn't take long before the eighth-grade boys—nearly adults to us—invent a game in which they take great delight. They discover that if they chase the first-grade girls, they can eventually corner us in a small "L" of the building where the tall red cedars hide what happens. Once we are herded into the corner, the boys flip up our beautiful circle skirts. Helpless against their taunts and physical presence, we cry.

I see the red brick of the schoolhouse as we huddle there, sometimes all four of us girls at once. Nothing grows in the shade of the tall cedars; the dirt is powder, dusting our once clean shoes. We cry and beg as we maneuver to hold down our skirts. They encircle us. There is no way out. They are so much bigger and have blocked every exit. Our beautiful circle skirts we love so much, made with loving care by our overworked and loving mothers, are weapons in the hands of bullies, used against us, every recess, every day.

I can't recall what triggered this thought, but I remember the clear resolve it brought. Sitting in the church basement during a Sunday School class, I am struck by a revelation: they *want* us to cry! And it follows: I will not let them have their way. The next day, I am determined to try out my plan. Again, I am cornered by the boys between the red cedars and the red bricks. I look directly at the bricks, then at the boys. I am afraid, hardly daring to breath. I bite my lip. I wait.

It takes only a few days of holding to my plan before I overhear one of the boys say to the others who are chasing me, "Don't bother with her. She won't cry anyway." They stop. I was right.

I gather the girls. "They *want* us to cry. If we don't, they'll go away." Just like that, we all give up crying. Eventually, the boys move on to some new recess pastime. And the story is etched in my mind: *Don't ever let them see you cry.* It was clear to me that, to be safe, I should hide my emotions. This was how the world worked.

I found confirmation for my story many times over decades, never more than in large corporations where I was one of a few female executives among a host of men. My story aligned well with an overarching cultural story in nearly every place I worked. Conversations of the heart were seldom honored. (What do the terms *human resources, human capital,* or *manpower* suggest to you?) For decades, I did not see that I had created a story, nor did I recall its origin. To be successful and safe in the world: *Hide your heart.* To me it was not a hypothesis. It was true.

It took years of additional exploration for me to discover that I was locked into a story that was no longer serving me. I love the shy and frightened first-grader who figured out how to protect herself and her friends in a situation that should never have happened. I'm grateful for how she persevered. Now I can free her up to be a child with a story instead of charging her with responsibility for shaping the rest of my life.

■ ■ ■

We all have created such stories. They grow out of our experiences and become our view of *how the world really is.* We often construct stories to protect us from a world we cannot comprehend. A story of life crafted by a six-year-old can be as strong as steel as it becomes embedded in and reinforced by the way we live our lives. Unexamined, our stories take on the patina of truth. Because they serve us well in many situations, we do not think to question them, to wonder if they are being overused, or to explore whether they are too small for who we are becoming. It's important for each of us to critically and compassionately explore those personal stories that limit possibilities. When we hear the voice of our younger self pronouncing "the truth," we might try to trace the origin of its insistence. We can honor our lifelong stories for how they helped us in the past and invite them to become a part of our history, not our present.

Of course, it's not only our personal stories that must be replaced to live more fully in edge times. Stories inherent in the fabric of modernity must be challenged.

Climate and biodiversity loss have already shifted the landscape beneath our feet. Lives hang in the balance. It's well past time to exorcise exhausted and harmful cultural stories that portray the living world as inanimate, separate, strictly competitive, or lacking intelligence, purpose, and agency. Stories about humans that give preference to entitlement, superiority, independence, or heroics must be replaced. We already know how such stories will end, for the entire Earth is living and dying with the results.

Throughout this book, we have discussed alternative stories, personal examples, and the results of scientific studies that debunk these limiting, often damning, cultural falsehoods prevalent in modernity. But let's be clear: even blatantly specious cultural stories are deeply embedded and pernicious. Why? Who or what do they serve? Look carefully. Many stories that give priority to the human species and promote *othering* enable the dominant culture to avoid discomfort or inconvenience and preserve the wealth and power of the privileged. Ridding ourselves of such deeply embedded stories may be lonely work; replacing certainty with curiosity is no easy feat and is not likely to be welcomed by many.

We can begin the difficult and important work of challenging our time-honored stories through the practice of a long, loving look at the real, gazing on what is without judging or fixing. As we keep returning to our truest selves, our soul essence, we can hold our "once certain truth" in the light of increasing awareness and understanding of our place in relationship to the living world. As we continue to reweave our connections to Earth, we will be drawn into the wisdom inherent in *her* stories. In that space, entrenched worldviews begin to release their hold on us.

In the beginning of this book, I wrote that climate change, ecosystem loss, and species extinction reflect an individual and collective spiritual crisis. We have become unmoored from our place in the family of things, we have forgotten our soul connections. We do not make this journey alone, and yet this is a personal journey to reweave soul and Earth, to create new stories to live by that remind us that everything belongs, and everything is sacred.

Early on, I invited you to a pilgrimage like no other. This is it. We do not know our destination; we never will. All we know is that we must begin. The path will be made by walking. As we discern what steps to take along the rocky edge, we will join with others in sharing stories of connection and kinship and a hope for mutual flourishing.

■ ■ ■

Darkness envelopes us as we walk without a word along the trail illuminated only by the faint red light held by our guide. Fresh snow crunches under our feet and sends up waves of cold, colder even than the predawn temperatures, hovering in the teens. A harsh call shatters the silence, so close. High overhead an echoed response and the beating of wings. We have driven for two days and over 1,300 miles from our home in West Virginia to be here, in the middle of Nebraska, to witness the annual migration of sandhill cranes.

Each spring from March to mid-April, half a million or more cranes leave their winter homes in Texas and New Mexico to fly north. Squeezed into an hourglass flight path, they congregate here on an eighty-mile section of the Platte River to rebuild their strength for the next leg of their journey. Feeding on plants, invertebrates, reptiles, and small rodents from the nearby wet meadows and waste corn from the surrounding farm fields, they will increase their body weight by twenty percent to prepare for travel to their summer homes across Canada or even as far as Alaska and Siberia.

Cranes have lived on Earth longer than most other birds. Fossils of their relatives dating back ten million years have been discovered. This specific migration path in the center of North America has been used by cranes for many thousands and possibly millions of years. Sandhill cranes and the Platte River forged a relationship that began 10,000 to 12,000 years ago when the river formed after the last ice age.

Cranes roost sans trees in the shallowest part of the river. The Platte is a braided river, deepest along the edges with shallows and sandbars in the middle. By putting deeper water between themselves and hungry foxes or coyotes, cranes receive ample warning as predators are forced to splash their way toward a potential dinner.

Because cranes are legally hunted in 49 states, they are easily frightened by flashes and sudden noises, so we remain in silence as we enter the specially constructed viewing blind where we, like the birds, await dawn. From three to over four feet tall, these gray birds have long, dark, pointed bills and white cheeks punctuated by bright red foreheads. As the sky begins to lighten, they make unique patterns above us, with their necks extended and long legs trailing behind. Gradually, they raise their voices until it seems as if every bird is participating in a toccata and fugue in an unnamable key. Perhaps they bugle for the pure joy of making sound. Or maybe to let friends know, "I'm alive! I made it through the night!"

The sky brightens, and more birds take flight. Hundreds fly overhead, crisscrossing the sky while hundreds, thousands, more glide in the opposite direction. Back and forth, cranes transect the sky, the sight and sound unlike anything we have known. We are enveloped in a tumult of wings and resounding calls.

If "hope is a thing with feathers,"[2] as poet Emily Dickinson wrote, what could be more hopeful than a sky full of sandhill cranes who each year follow the same path with certainty born of a wisdom we cannot comprehend? What could be more inspiring than a relationship between a river and a species, forged over tens of thousands of years?

And yet. I could write about the extensive human intervention that has changed the course and function of the river so that it is no longer the diverse ecosystem it once was. I could tell you about the thousands of acres of genetically modified corn fields that draw water from the Platte and drain the immense Ogalala Aquifer below. We could discuss the geese who have moved into the area and are competing with the cranes for food. All that is real too. Is this a migration story of hope? Or a reminder of how much has already been lost and is still failing?

■ ■ ■

"Where do I find hope?" I am asked this question time and again as I lead retreats and seminars where we face squarely into the daunting challenges of our species and our Earth family. It's impossible to answer that question without first considering what we mean by *hope*. On one end of the spectrum, people sometimes embrace a kind of blind hope grounded in ignoring reality; at the other end of the continuum, some have abandoned hope entirely. I believe that there are other options in this Goldilocks scenario. How we define hope is our story—and therefore a choice. What story will offer potential and possibility for you and the future? Let's explore this in more detail.

Ignoring science and direct experience to claim that the future will be like the present is to envision hope as a kind of magic fairy dust that has the power to create what we'd like to experience. And isn't that tempting? We look at a clear-cut forest and hope that newly planted trees will replace the old. We add solar panels to our homes and businesses and hope the change will address climate chaos. Hope untethered to reality is fantasy. More trees may be planted on the clear-cut land of a once-lush forest, but the ecosystem that thrived there will not recover for centuries, if ever. Solar panels can help reduce fossil fuel consumption, but they do not come close to offsetting our collective lifestyle, no matter how much we hope they will.

It is dangerous to conflate hope with magic. Our souls do not grow in depth or connection when we fail to bear witness to our own losses and those of others. Without looking with love on what is, just as it is, we deny the fullness of life. What's more, a Pollyanna view prevents us from taking action that could save lives, including our own.

At the other end of the continuum, we may refuse to see any hope for the present or future. In this case, we might say that there is no use trying, for nothing we do will matter anyway. We choose resignation or despair. Given lackluster responses to the latest environmental reports from both governments and citizens, it's easy to understand this feeling. And it's partially true; it is too late for many of the things we might once have done to allay harm to this world.

Yet, in giving up all hope, we assume that we can comprehend all that is possible, that we can *know* what the future holds. Earth is endowed with wisdom and genius beyond our understanding, and Earth has agency. This Earth, this miraculous creation of the cosmos, 4.5 billion years old, has evolved and survived five previous mass extinctions. Yes, there seems to be little doubt that our world will change substantially from what we have known. And many of us fear what the change will bring. I do. Still, we cannot know what moments of beauty and wonder may be tucked into the corners of edge times. We cannot fathom if what appears strange, uncomfortable, or dangerous today may hold a silver lining now hidden from us. And we cannot comprehend the ways in which Earth herself may respond to changes.

When we deny hope, we deny our soul's calling, our unique purpose that is aligned with this time and place. Perhaps we imagine that cynicism will shield us from disappointment and heartbreak. But without embarking on our soul journey and offering our contributions to the world, we stunt our spiritual growth and risk living a life cut off from deeper purpose and meaning. We leave the world without the benefit of the gifts with which we have been endowed for just this time.

Somewhere along the spectrum of hope we look realistically at the loss already suffered and acknowledge that it is only beginning. And we find within ourselves the commitment to work toward a life-affirming future, understanding that Earth has agency and is weaving a new tapestry. We look into the face of grief and loss as we acknowledge that the future holds possibilities beyond our knowing.

Several months ago, it seemed that the Great Salt Lake was dying. Now a record snowy winter has jump-started a potential recovery. Although there is no guarantee that water conservation efforts will be expanded to support the return of this vital ecosystem, what looked to be impossible has become possible if we collaborate with the opportunity that Earth is offering. Of course, collaboration does not involve organizing a response based on what we think is best for other beings. Indeed, in edge times, we may be called to followership more frequently than to leadership. And sometimes, we just need to get out of the way to allow for what is unfolding.

Writer Cal Flyn offers numerous examples of how desecrated areas where human activities have been prohibited are rebounding.[3] Searching out locations such as the buffer zone in Cyprus or the ruins of Chernobyl, she has traveled to a dozen places of desolation and decay; in most, humans are forbidden. Surprisingly, many have become habitats for endangered species, a refuge for wildness. Far from restored, these lands have been forever poisoned, terraformed, and abandoned. Yet somehow the living world is reshaping these places, enabling them to hold both death and fecundity.

Because we will never know of outcomes beyond our lifetime, we can choose to live in a story that is grounded in the real and that still offers greater possibility. Living with hope is a choice. When we choose hope, we embrace what is already unfolding and discern if and how we are called to respond. Without any illusion that the path will be easy, we choose to live more fully into our soul's mission and offer our gifts to the world guided by Earth's wisdom.

■ ■ ■

So, is the story of the sandhill cranes and the Platte River a story of hope or a reminder of how much we are losing?

And what of Flyn's findings that disasters can be at least partially transformed into areas that support life? Perhaps a simple practice might help us hold what appear to be contradictions in these edge times. *Both...And...*

I often catch myself joining two seemingly opposing thoughts with *but. How amazing and wonderful that sandhill cranes continue to follow an ancient migration path,* but *we are destroying so much of the ecosystem of the Platte River upon which they depend.* "But" can negate and drain joy and hope from the first portion of that statement. It implies that I would be foolish to celebrate this vast migration. It places a valid concern about ecosystem loss at greater significance than the miracle of the sandhill cranes.

We might find it challenging in these edge times to allow ourselves, encourage ourselves, to rejoice in beauty, abundance, and joy. Yet, our hearts and souls are fed by opening to the gifts of this amazing, miraculous world even as we bear witness to the losses. *We have destroyed so much of the ecosystem of the Platte River on which sandhill cranes depend,* and *how amazing and wonderful that cranes are still following an ancient migration path.*

The old woman sits and considers. Then she begins weaving anew a garment of great beauty. She is vigilant to stir the cauldron of seeds to populate the world. And the black dog is ever-present, ready to tear again at the threads, creating chaos. *Both . . . and . . .* Wisdom teachers remind us that this is the way of the world. Marvel at the beauty. Weep at the loss. Wait patiently for the next pattern to emerge. Our hearts must hold it all. Fortunately, they can.

Perhaps this need for *both/and* is why our work must begin with gratitude. We are still awash in gifts. We live because life on this Earth evolved over hundreds of millions of years to enable a world of vitality and liveliness. We are fed, sheltered, and clothed from the gifts of sunshine photosynthesized by plants. The average adult human body is 50 to 65 percent water.

We remember the most basic gift: air. Breathe in and thank the trees. Our lungs fill with oxygen because of these giants, keystones of the forest ecosystem and home to an abundance of species. Take another breath and thank the phytoplankton, those tiny plants that live on the surface of oceans and lakes. Phytoplankton are the base of marine and freshwater food webs and key players in the carbon cycle. They provide half of the world's oxygen production and account for 20 percent of the oxygen in our biosphere even though they account for only about 1 percent of the global plant biomass. "That's a higher percentage than all of the tropical rainforests on land combined." [4]

Incredible gifts! If we are not stopped in our tracks by the wonder of these miracles, we aren't paying attention. To pay attention fully is to be flooded with gratitude. As Robin Wall Kimmerer reminds us, "Even a wounded world is feeding us. Even a wounded world holds us, giving us moments of wonder and joy." [5]

Hope will not be presented to us on a silver platter. Hope is not coming to us from others. You must choose it. Bear witness to loss, gaze in awe and wonder, gratefully receive Earth's gifts, and offer what it yours to give. Make the soul journey to the essence of your true self, deepen communion with the sacred world, discern what is calling you in the moment. Recognize that you live within a beautiful web of life, primed for mutual flourishing and that Earth has agency and wisdom beyond your knowing. Live fully alive to what is in these edge times while following the thread of Earth's dream to what could be.

■ ■ ■

Perhaps we might ponder further the story of the old woman weaving the tapestry of the world. Remember that the elders shared this story for times such as these. It is a story of remarkable and beautiful creativity born from the chaos of destruction, of the necessity of old ways dying to make way for transformation, of the power of letting go of what has been to begin again, and of tending seeds— those tiny and powerful repositories of life for future generations.

Writer and historian Rebecca Solnit asks us to consider what we're afraid of giving up in the climate crisis and then turns the question on its head to ask us to consider another possibility. What if the changing future means "… giving up things we're well rid of, from deadly emissions to nagging feelings of doom and complicity in destruction? What if the austerity is how we live now—and the abundance could be what is to come?"[6] What if? What if the old woman might weave a garment that is richer, more beautiful, and filled with even greater vitality than the present times of modernity to which we are clinging?

Might we imagine such a future where humans live in simple abundance, where joy is found in clean water, healthy food, and community connections? Where our work aligns with our soul calling and brings deep satisfaction? Where grief is shared so that no one weeps alone? Where kith and kin are acknowledged and honored members of the diverse Earth community? Where the threads of soul and Earth have been rewoven so that we thrive in communion? Where more attention is given to the well-being of future generations than the desires of our own?

What stories might you be invited to leave behind so that you can open more fully to a future with such possibility? What newly evolving stories will guide you into the rich and beautiful essence of your soul? We live in edge times, embroiled in the chaos of destruction and creation. Return to the deep, claim your new beginning, and with vibrant threads reweave soul and Earth. Live fully alive within the sacred and ever-renewing web of life, sharing joy, grief, and hope. Place steppingstones toward mutual thriving to ease the way for future generations. Reconnect Earth and soul to live fully alive amid the chaos, collaborating for a future that beckons from beyond what we can possibly imagine.

Questions for Book Group Discussions

Note for book groups from the author: I am fan of book groups and participate in one myself. I'd be honored if you were to choose my book for your group and would be glad to join you for 30 minutes by Zoom to discuss *Earth & Soul: Reconnecting amid Climate Chaos*. If you are interested, please make the request via www.leahmoranrampy .com. I wish you rich discussions.   —*Leah Rampy*

1. The Introduction begins with the story of the old woman weaving the world. This story reappears throughout the book as a metaphor for our times. Does the story feel relevant to you as you reflect on the world today? Are we living within a beautifully woven tapestry, or one being pulled apart? Is the old woman still pondering what to do next or has she begun reweaving a new world? Consider the meaning of the dog and the pot of seeds. Are there any lessons from this ancient story that might offer guidance for us in these times? For you personally?

2. Rampy shares stories of her early childhood in Kansas and how she felt connected to the land, trees, and plants there. Can you recall a time in the past when you felt deeply connected to the living world around you? What feelings arise as you recall this scenario? Or if you have no memories of such a time, how does that feel to you? What was your most recent experience of connection? Does connection matter to you?

3. What is your reaction to the birthing of the cosmos that has brought forth such a diverse array of plant and animal life? Does this make a case for the kinship of all beings? Rampy explores her own potential loss of kith and kin through frequent moves to different locales. Do you feel related to the land and beings around you? What do you think about Robin Wall Kimmerer's quote that it's possible to become indigenous to a place if we live and care for it as if our lives depend on it? In what ways might becoming indigenous matter?

4. Rampy makes a distinction between connection and communion, the latter being a wordless heart-to-heart exchange. Why is communion important for living amid climate chaos?

5. What examples do you see of how we have frayed connections with Earth? Rampy writes, "How do we cope when we are heartachingly lonely for the ecology that feeds our soul, but we do not even realize that this relationship is the one for which we long?" How do you respond to this question?

6. The author cites research to show specific health benefits of time outdoors and goes on to explore even more gifts available to us when we "come to our senses." Recall an experience of being in the natural world with your senses fully alive, receiving awe and wonder. How would you respond to the question the author poses: "Why take time in our busy lives to slow our pace, to allow the space to receive awe and wonder?"

7. In Chapter 6, you're invited to create a mobius strip to symbolize weaving a life where wonder and joy are embraced along with sorrow and loss. Rampy posits that you cannot fully hold what we consider to be positive emotions without also bearing witness to loss. Reflect on examples from your own life to probe the truth of this premise. Share what feels right for you.

8. Thomas Berry coined the term *inscendence* to describe the inward journey to the depths of our soul. He believed (as does the author) that to live fully alive we must probe the depths of our being to come to an understanding of who we truly are meant to be in this place and time, connected to this Earth. Yet sometimes in that soul space, everything is obscured, we feel lost and can sense no way forward. The invitation is to wait in darkness until the next step, one we cannot yet imagine, is revealed. Waiting patiently without action is countercultural and perhaps counterintuitive. What support might we need for such times in the dark night of the soul? Where might we turn for such support?

9. We live in a world of geniuses, surrounded by beings with intelligence that is varied, deep, and often beyond our human way of understanding. If we fully accept that statement, does it change how we interact with other beings? How can we free ourselves from the cultural paradigm that claims humans as *the* exceptional species? What is the cost of not trying?

10. Do you sense that our species is currently on the threshold, poised between a world we once knew and unknown possibilities? What does it feel like to be on the edge? Do you sense that this is a time of peril, opportunity, or both? Can you sense what is waiting to be born in you? In us? In cosmic time?

11. Rampy quotes her mentor as saying, "Everyone is a leader at the point of their gifts." Where are you being called to step into leadership? Might contemplative leadership allow you to draw on deeper wisdom and greater possibilities for the challenges that lie ahead?

12. What story will you choose to live into that might lay steppingstones toward a future of mutual thriving?

Acknowledgments

We live within a web of beings without whom we could not thrive. I am particularly grateful to be part of a community that has offered such gracious and stalwart support to me in the writing of this book. From beginning to end, I am blessed with a family who believed in me. The love and support of my parents was never in doubt; even when they didn't understand some of the choices I made throughout my life, they always offered unconditional love. I miss you dearly, Mom and Dad.

My husband, David Rampy, has always affirmed whatever star I chose to follow and came along for the ride without complaint. We've enjoyed a lifetime of adventuring together. For decades he whispered to me, "You need to write a book!" When I finally took his advice, he ensured that I had time to write when it seemed impossible. He read many versions of these chapters before they were touched by an editor and didn't hesitate to ask probing questions. Thank you, David. This book would not have happened without your ongoing love and partnership.

For Andrew Rampy and Ana Rampy, I love you so much and ache for you and the world we are leaving to you. Beyond all the protests, climate training, and EPA or DEP testimonies we've participated in as a family, this book is my best effort to offer possibilities for your future. Thank you both for always supporting me. Ana, thank you for allowing me to share a part of your story in these pages. I honor your courage.

The friendship and support of Leslie Williams, poet and soul friend, has meant so much. You listened to some of my first efforts and reminded me that I was called to write this book. Thank you for sharing this journey.

Beth Norcross, founder of the *Center for Spirituality in Nature,* invited me to be a part of the leadership team and to join in the important work of the Center. What a highlight to co-author and co-lead with you the six-part program *The Spiritual Wisdom of Trees.* Thank you for your steady encouragement and affirmation throughout the writing process and beyond.

Early chapters of this book were read with care and attention by the extraordinary communications guru and friend, Rebecca Leet. Your feedback helped me to hone my writing skills, and you made me feel that I could do this. Thank you for so generously offering your time and wisdom to further this book.

Friends and neighbors Claudia Giannini, Donna Hiatt, Lindsay McLaughlin, and Kay Schultz became my very first group of readers and spent hours together discussing the themes, affirming what worked, and identifying what was unclear. I am so grateful for your time, wisdom, and support. Thank you. And friend and editor, Leslie Miller, a deep bow for volunteering to help me proofread this book. The entire book was greatly enhanced by your commitment, expertise, and care. Truthfully, the errors remaining are all mine.

Dear friends and colleagues from *Shalem Institute*, I learned so much from you about contemplative living and leadership over the years we worked together. Special thanks to Carole Crumley, my partner in new endeavors and pilgrimage leader extraordinaire who taught me so much; Ann Dean, my wonderful mentor and colleague; Liz Ward and Tilden Edwards, who consistently brought depth to any conversation; and to all of you for our collaboration to better understand and explain contemplative leadership. I treasure our friendship and continue to draw on your wisdom. Any misunderstandings of contemplative leadership are my own.

For all those who've participated in retreats, pilgrimages, seminars, peer groups, classes, and Church of the Wild Two Rivers gatherings that I've led, I've learned so much from our interactions. Thank you for allowing me to offer content and practices on this topic so dear to me and for helping me hone my understanding of what it means to live in fuller relationships within this amazing world. I am in your debt. And for every co-leader I've been privileged to work with along the way, I'm grateful for all I've learned from you.

I'm fortunate to be part of a village where we have ongoing discussions about climate and ecology and where we care about native plants, soil health, the small water cycle, local food, and permaculture. Thanks to Todd and Susan Lewis for engaging in a conversation about the meaning of soul. To all in this community, I benefit greatly from the richness of our discussions and value all the encouragement I've received for my personal journey. Thank you, Shepherd Village.

To the many excellent authors and leaders who have shaped my understanding of our current situation, thank you. Many of your names are referenced in this book. Your work makes a difference to us all. How fortunate I am to live a short walk from Shepherdstown's Four Seasons Books, our local independent bookstore that supports the work of authors mentioned herein and that of local authors.

A special tip of the hat to the folks at *Bio4Climate* for all the resources they provide and for personally showing me years ago how critical biodiversity is to the flourishing of all.

I'm grateful to the staff at Bold Story Press who help to broaden the impact of women's voices. Thanks to Emily Barrosse, Nedah Rose, Christine O'Connor, Karen Polaski, and Cathy Bamji who worked to manifest this book.

We are all blessed to live in an amazing world of beauty and wisdom. Places such as Iona, Scotland; the Olympic Peninsula in Washington state; Newfoundland; Australia; South America; and many others, along with the beings who inhabit these ecosystems, have made my life rich in beauty and wonder. In truth, there is no life without you. For the Indigenous peoples of these lands who have long cared for kith and kin and offered wisdom to the world, we are all deeply in your debt.

Last, but by no means least, thank you to the plants and critters just outside my door and the two dogs who live within. I hope I remember to bow in gratitude for your sacred presence every day. We live because of you. May we remember that.

Endnotes

INTRODUCTION

1 John Philip Newell, *Sacred Earth Sacred Souls; Celtic Wisdom for Reawakening to What Our Soul Know and Healing the World* (New York: HarperOne, 2021), 3–4.

2 Michael Meade, *Why the World Doesn't End; Tales of Renewal in Times of Loss* (Seattle, WA: GreenFire Press, 2012), 49–56.

3 Joel Makower, "Climate Change and the New Language of Weather | Greenbiz," accessed August 20, 2023, https://www.greenbiz.com/article/climate-change-and-new-language-weather.

4 Michael Vescio, "The Historic Derecho of June 29, 2012," Department of Commerce, accessed August 10, 2023, https://www.weather.gov/media/publications/assessments/derecho12.pdf.

5 Jason Samenow, "Lightning Gone Wild during D.C.'s Derecho," Washington Post (blog), June 29, 2023, https://www.washingtonpost.com/blogs/capital-weather-gang/post/lightning-gone-wild-during-dcs-derecho/2012/07/02/gJQACeuqIW_blog.html.

6 Casey McNerthney, "Heat Wave Broils Western Washington, Shattering Seattle and Regional," accessed August 20, 2023, https://www.historylink.org/File/21266.

7 Sarah Kaplan and Andrew Ba Tran, "Nearly 1 in 3 Americans Experienced a Weather Disaster This Summer," Washington Post, September 4, 2021, https://www.washingtonpost.com/climate-environment/2021/09/04/climate-disaster-hurricane-ida/.

8 Zach Levitt and Bonnie Berkowitz, "Cold, Heat, Fires, Hurricanes and Tornadoes: The Year in Weather Disasters," Washington Post, accessed August 20, 2023, https://www.washingtonpost.com/nation/interactive/2021/weather-disasters-2021/.

9 Devika Reo, "The Extreme Weather Events of 2023," The Week, accessed August 31, 2023, https://theweek.com/in-depth/1021278/2023-extreme-weather.

10 Rebecca Lindsay, "Climate Change: Atmospheric Carbon Dioxide | NOAA Climate.gov," accessed August 20, 2023, http://www.climate.gov/news-features/understanding-climate/climate-change-atmospheric-carbon-dioxide.

11 Claire O'Shea, "NASA Clocks July 2023 as Hottest Month on Record Ever Since 1880," Text, NASA, August 14, 2023, http://www.nasa.gov/press-release/nasa-clocks-july-2023-as-hottest-month-on-record-ever-since-1880·

12 Atmospheric Moisture Increase | Climate Signals," accessed August 20, 2023, https://www.climatesignals.org/climate-signals/atmospheric-moisture-increase#more.

13 "Secretary-General Calls Latest IPCC Climate Report 'Code Red for Humanity', Stressing 'Irrefutable' Evidence of Human Influence | UN Press," accessed August 20, 2023, https://press.un.org/en/2021/sgsm20847.doc.htm.

14 Jessica Blunden, "Reporting on the State of the Climate in 2020 | NOAA Climate.gov," accessed August 20, 2023, http://www.climate.gov/news-features/understanding-climate/reporting-state-climate-2020.

15 "Why We Need a Healthy Planet," accessed August 20, 2023, https://livingplanet.panda.org/en-US/impact.

16 "WWF—Building a Future in Which Humans Live in Harmony with Nature," accessed August 20, 2023, https://wwf.panda.org/.

17 Damian Carrington, "Just 3% of World's Ecosystems Remain Intact, Study Suggests," The Guardian, April 15, 2021, sec. Environment, https://www.theguardian.com/environment/2021/apr/15/just-3-of-worlds-ecosystems-remain-intact-study-suggests.

18 "The State of the World's Forests 2020," www.fao.org, accessed August 31, 2023, https://doi.org/10.4060/CA8642EN.

19 Joe Simmons, SJ, "'Where Is the Love?' Or 'Prayer: A Long Loving Look at the Real'—The Jesuit Post," January 29, 2012, https://thejesuitpost.org/2012/01/where -is-the-love-or-prayer-a-long-loving-look-at-the-real/.

ONE: CONNECTIONS

1 Martin Luther King, "Christmas Sermon on Peace," (Ebenezer Baptist Church, Atlanta, GA, December 24, 1964), https://speakola.com/ideas/martin-luther-king-jr -interconnected-world-massey-5-1967.

2 "Five Oaks for the Kansas Landscape," Dyck Arboretum, October 29, 2014, https://dyckarboretum.org/five-oaks-for-kansas/.

3 hsotr, "A Forest in Western Kansas," *Homestead on the Range* (blog), September 30, 2014, https://homesteadontherange .com/2014/09/30/a-forest-in-western-kansas/.

4 "The Pros and Cons of the Eastern Redcedar | Piedmont Master Gardeners," accessed January 6, 2022, https://piedmontmastergardeners.org/article/the-pros-and -cons-of-the-eastern-redcedar/.

5 "Eastern Red Cedar Berries—LocalHarvest," accessed January 6, 2022, https://www.localharvest.org/ark/eastern -red-cedar-berries.

6 "The Pros and Cons of the Eastern Redcedar | Piedmont Master Gardeners."

7 Suzanne Simard, *Finding the Mother Tree; Discovering the Wisdom of the Forest* (New York: Alfred P. Knopf, 2021), 153–65.

8 Simard, 153–65.

9 "Suzanne Simard—Forests Are Wired For Wisdom," The On Being Project, accessed January 2, 2022, https://onbeing.org/ programs/suzanne-simard-forests-are-wired-for-wisdom/.

10 Merlin Sheldrake, *Entangled Life; How Fungi Make Our Worlds, Change Our Minds & Shape Our Futures* (New York: Random House, 2020), 4.

11 Sheldrake, 154.

12 Meg Lohman, *The Arbornaut; A Life Discovering the Eighth Continent in the Trees Above Us* (New York: Farrar, Straus, and Giroux, 2021), 156.

13 Lohman, 203.

14 Rick Bass, "The Larch," in *Old Growth; The Best Writing about Trees from Orion Magazine* (Northhampton, MA: Orion Magazine, 2021), 72.

15 Sheldrake, *Entangled Life; How Fungi Make Our Worlds, Change Our Minds & Shape Our Futures*, 6.

16 Douglas W. Tallamy, *Nature's Best Hope; A New Approach to Conservation That Starts in Your Yard* (Portland, OR: Timber Press, Inc., 2019), 144.

17 "West Virginia Northern Flying Squirrel," accessed May 8, 2022, https://www.biologicaldiversity.org/species/mammals /West_Virginia_northern_flying_squirrel/index.html.

18 Diana Beresford-Kroeger, *To Speak for the Trees; My Life's Journey from Ancient Celtic Wisdom to a Healing Vision of the Forest* (Toronto: Random House Canada, 2019).

19 David George Haskell, *The Forest Unseen: A Year's Watch in Nature* (New York: Penguin Books, 2012).

TWO: KITH & KIN

1 Lyanda Lynn Haupt, *Rooted; Life at the Crossroads of Science, Nature, and Spirit* (New York: Little, Brown Spark, 2021), 24.

2 "Noxious Weed | Russell County, KS," accessed August 20, 2023, https://russellcountykansas.com/201/Noxious-Weed.

3 Robin Wall Kimmerer, *Braiding Sweetgrass; Indigenous Wisdom, Scientific Knowledge, and the Teachings of Plants* (Minneapolis, MN: Milkweed Editions, 2013), 47.

4 Jack D. Forbes, "Indigenous Americans: Spirituality and Ecos," American Academy of Arts & Sciences, Fall 2021, https://www.amacad.org/publication/indigenous-americans-spirituality-and-ecos.

5 Enrique Salmon, "Kincentric Ecology: Indigenous Perceptions of the Human-Nature Relationship," *Ecological Applications* 10, no. 5 (October 2000): 1327, https://doi .org/10.2307/2641288.

6 Forbes, "Indigenous Americans: Spirituality and Ecos."

7 Gavin Van Horn, Robin Wall Kimmerer, and John Hausdoerffer, eds., *Kinship; Belonging in a World of Relations*, vol. 01, Planet, 05 vols. (Libertyville, IL: Center for Humans and Nature Press, 2021).

8 "Cosmic Calendar," February 18, 2022, https://en.wikipedia.org
   /wiki/Cosmic_Calendar.

9 "Cosmic Calendar."

10 Class notes taken during The Emerging New Cosmology
   taught by Larry Edwards, October 2017, at the Fox
   Institute for Creation Spirituality. For more information
   see Larry's work here. http://www.thegreatstory.org
   /CosmicWalk.pdf

11 Steve Paulson, "Living in Mystery" In Interview with Marcelo
   Gleiser," in *Kinship; Belonging in a World of Relationships*,
   vol. 1, Planet (Libertyville, IL: Center for Humans and Nature
   Press, 2021), 74.

12 "Witless Bay Ecological Reserve—Environment and Climate
   Change," October 23, 2020, https://www.gov.nl.ca/ecc
   /natural-areas/wer/r-wbe/.

13 Amitav Ghosh, *The Nutmeg's Curse; Parables for a Planet in
   Crisis* (Chicago: University of Chicago Press, 2021), 198.

14 Sheldrake, *Entangled Life; How Fungi Make Our Worlds, Change
   Our Minds & Shape Our Futures*, 16.

15 Ghosh, *The Nutmeg's Curse; Parables for a Planet in Crisis*, 81.

16 Wall Kimmerer, *Braiding Sweetgrass; Indigenous Wisdom,
   Scientific Knowledge, and the Teachings of Plants*, 9.

17 Ghosh, *The Nutmeg's Curse; Parables for a Planet in Crisis*, 53–55.

18 Wall Kimmerer, *Braiding Sweetgrass; Indigenous Wisdom,
   Scientific Knowledge, and the Teachings of Plants*, 9.

19 Patty Krawec, *Becoming Kin: An Indigenous Call to Unforgetting
   the Past and Reimagining Our Future* (Minneapolis, MN:
   Broadleaf Books, 2022), 22–23.

THREE: COMMUNION

1 Thomas Merton, *The Hidden Ground of Love; The Letters of
   Thomas Merton* (New York: Farrar, Straus, and Giroux, 2011), 13.

2 James A. Quinn, "An Abstract of The Journal of John Woolman,"
   accessed January 13, 2022, https://www.friendsjournal.org/
   legacy/abington/gwynedd/John_Woolman.html.

3 Thomas Merton, *Conjectures of a Guilty Bystander* (New York:
   Doubleday, 1966), 140–42.

4 Joshua J. Mark, "Hildegard of Bingen," in *World History Encyclopedia*, May 30, 2019, https://www.worldhistory.org /Hildegard_of_Bingen/.

5 Pierre Teilhard de Chardin, *The Divine Milieu* (New York: Harper Torch Books, 1960), 36.

6 Thomas Berry, *Evening Thoughts: Reflecting on Earth as a Sacred Community*, ed. Mary Evelyn Tucker, Reprint edition (San Francisco, CA: Counterpoint, 2015).

7 Thich Nat Hanh, "The Insight of Interbeing |," accessed September 1, 2023, https://www.garrisoninstitute.org/blog /insight-of-interbeing/.

8 Leath Tonino, "The Sun Magazine | The Egret Lifting From The River; David Hinton on the Wisdom of Ancient Chinese Poets | Issue 469," The Sun Magazine, January 2015, https://www .thesunmagazine.org/issues/469/the-egret-lifting-from-the-river.

9 David Abram, *The Spell of the Sensuous* (New York: Vintage Books, 1996).

10 Dacher Keltner, *Awe; The New Science of Everyday Wonder and How It Can Transform Your Life* (New York: Penguin Books, 2023), 33–34.

11 Bill Plotkin, *The Journey of Soul Initiation; A Field Guide for Visionaries, Evolutionaries, and Revolutionaries* (Novato, CA: New World Library, 2021), 7.

12 Thomas Berry, *The Dream of the Earth* (San Francisco, CA: Sierra Club Books, 1988), 207–8.

13 Plotkin, 17.

14 Stephen Harrod Buhner, *Earth Grief; The Journey into and through Ecological Loss* (Boulder, CO: Raven Press, 2022), 256.

15 Buhner, 256.

FOUR: TATTERED CONNECTIONS

1 Maria Popova, "Barry Lopez on the Cure for Our Existential Loneliness and the Three Tenets of a Full Life," *The Marginalian* (blog), September 18, 2022, https://www .themarginalian.org/2022/09/18/barry-lopez-place-loneliness/.

2 Gareth Cook, "Why We Are Wired to Connect," *Scientific American*, October 22, 2013, https://www.scientificamerican .com/article/why-we-are-wired-to-connect/.

3 Linda Searing, "Loneliness Can Increase Risk of Heart Disease by 27 Percent for Older Women," *Washington Post*, accessed September 14, 2022, https://www.washingtonpost.com/health/2022/02/20/loneliness-heart-disease-older-women/.

4 David Derbyshire, "Loneliness Is a Killer: It's as Bad for Your Health as Alcoholism, Smoking and over-Eating, Say Sceintists," *Daily Mail*, July 28, 2010, https://www.dailymail.co.uk/health/article-1298225/Loneliness-killer-Its-bad-health-alcoholism-smoking-eating-say-scientists.html.

5 Christina Ianzito, "Former Surgeon General Vivek Murthy on Loneliness," AARP, accessed September 14, 2022, https://www.aarp.org/health/healthy-living/info-2020/vivek-murthy-loneliness.html.

6 Richard Louv, *Last Child in the Woods: Saving Our Children From Nature-Deficit Disorder.* (New York: Algonquin Books, 2008).

7 Rehema Figueiredo, "Children More Likely to Fall out of Bed than a Tree | Daily Mail Online," accessed September 14, 2022, https://www.dailymail.co.uk/news/article-3626687/Today-s-kids-likely-fall-bed-tree.html.

8 Wall Kimmerer, *Braiding Sweetgrass; Indigenous Wisdom, Scientific Knowledge, and the Teachings of Plants,* 156–166.

9 "How Has the Average Size of American Homes Changed over Time?," United States Now, accessed September 19, 2022, http://www.unitedstatesnow.org/how-has-the-average-size-of-american-homes-changed-over-time.htm.

10 "Self-Medicating in America," Niznik Behavioral Health, accessed September 19, 2022, https://www.niznikhealth.com/research-articles/self-medicating-in-america/.

11 "Time Spent with Media in the U.S. 2022," Statista, accessed May 17, 2023, https://www.statista.com/statistics/278544/time-spent-with-media-in-the-us/.

12 "Infographics—Screen Time vs. Lean Time | DNPAO | CDC," January 23, 2019, https://www.cdc.gov/nccdphp/dnpao/multimedia/infographics/getmoving.html.

13 Dara McAnulty, *Diary of a Young Naturalist* (Minneapolis, MN: Milkweed Editions, 2022), 198.

14 Ghosh, *The Nutmeg's Curse; Parables for a Planet in Crisis*, 36.

15 Ghosh, 37.

16 Ghosh, 39.

17 "Trail of Tears," *The Museum of the Cherokee Indian* (blog), accessed September 20, 2022, https://mci.org/archives/era/trail-of-tears.

18 Wall Kimmerer, *Braiding Sweetgrass; Indigenous Wisdom, Scientific Knowledge, and the Teachings of Plants*, 13.

19 Ghosh, *The Nutmeg's Curse; Parables for a Planet in Crisis*, 51.

20 Wall Kimmerer, *Braiding Sweetgrass; Indigenous Wisdom, Scientific Knowledge, and the Teachings of Plants*, 306.

21 Joanna Macy. *Coming Back to Life; The Updated Guide to the Work that Reconnects* (Gabriola Island, BC: New Society Publishers, 2014) 5.

22 Meade, *Why the World Doesn't End; Tales of Renewal in Times of Loss*, 62–64.

FIVE: COMING TO OUR SENSES

1 Thomas Berry and Mary Evelyn Tucker, *The Sacred Universe: Earth, Spirituality, and Religion in the Twenty-First Century* (Columbia University Press, 2009).

2 "Mistaken Point Ecological Reserve and UNESCO World Heritage Site," Environment and Climate Change, accessed September 1, 2022, https://www.gov.nl.ca/ecc/natural-areas/wer/r-mpe/.

3 "Mistaken Point Ecological Reserve and UNESCO World Heritage Site."

4 Steven Morris, "Back to Nature: 'Secret Garden' Outings Used to Aid Coronavirus Recovery," *The Guardian*, May 5, 2020, sec. World news, https://www.theguardian.com/world/2020/may/05/back-to-nature-secret-garden-outings-used-to-aid-coronavirus-recovery.

5 "Shinrin-Yoku: The Simple and Intuitive Form of Preventative Care," *Portland Japanese Garden* (blog), August 15, 2022, https://japanesegarden.org/2022/08/15/shinrin-yoku/.

6 "Forest Bathing: What It Is and Why You Should Try It," *Thrive*, accessed September 1, 2022, https://thrive.kaiserpermanente.org/thrive-together/live-well/forest-bathing-try.

7 Beresford-Kroeger, *To Speak for the Trees; My Life's Journey from Ancient Celtic Wisdom to a Healing Vision of the Forest*, 168.

8 Wohlleben, *The Hidden Language of Trees; What They Feel, How They Communicate*, trans. Jane Billinghurst (Berkeley, CA: Greystone Books, 2015), 7.

9 Wohlleben, 7–12.

10 Wohlleben, 223.

11 Wall Kimmerer, *Braiding Sweetgrass; Indigenous Wisdom, Scientific Knowledge, and the Teachings of Plants*, 111.

12 Brother David Steindl-Rast, *Words of Common Sense for Mind, Body and Soul* (West Conshohocken, PA: Templeton Press, 2002), 10.

13 "Science Explains 12 Benefits of Keeping a Gratitude Journal," accessed August 30, 2022, https://www.powerofpositivity.com/science-explains-12-benefits-gratitude-journal/.

14 Miriam MacGillis and Rhonda Fabian, "An Interview with Sister Miriam Therese MacGillis at Genesis Farm," *Kosmos Journal* (blog), Summer 2017, https://www.kosmosjournal.org/article/an-interview-with-sister-miriam-therese-macgillis-at-genesis-farm/.

SIX: DANCING WITH GRIEF & JOY

1 Joanna Macy, *World as Lover, World as Self.* (Berkeley, CA: Parallax Press, 1991).

2 Ruth Maclean and Dionne Searcey, "Congo to Auction Land to Oil Companies: 'Our Priority Is Not to Save the Planet,'" *The New York Times*, July 24, 2022, sec. World, https://www.nytimes.com/2022/07/24/world/africa/congo-oil-gas-auction.html.

3 John W. Reid and Thomas E. Lovejoy. *Ever Green; Saving Big Forests to Save the Planet.* (New York: W.W. Norton, 2022).

4 Verlyn Klinkenborg, "The Forest's Eye View," *The New York Review of Books* LXIX, no. 12 (July 21, 2022): 34.

5 "COP26: Landmark $500 Million Agreement Launched to Protect the DR Congo's Forest," *Africa Renewal*, November 10, 2021, https://www.un.org/africarenewal/magazine/december-2021/cop26-landmark-500-million-agreement-launched-protect-dr-congo%E2%80%99s-forest.

6 Maclean and Searcey, "Congo to Auction Land to Oil Companies."

7 "Majority of US Adults Believe Climate Change Is Most Important Issue Today," https://www.apa.org, accessed July 29, 2022, https://www.apa.org/news/press/releases/2020/02/climate-change.

8 "UCSF Sustainability," accessed July 29, 2022, https://sustainability.ucsf.edu/1.830.

9 "UCSF Sustainability."

10 Constance Fitzgerald, OCD, "Impasse and Dark Night" (Washington, DC: Shalem Institute for Spiritual Formation, 2016), 2.

11 Joanna Macy and Chris Johnstone, *Active Hope; How to Face the Mess We're in without Going Crazy* (Novato, CA: New World Library, 2012), 37–39.

12 "CSC Communities – Creation Spirituality Is about Reawakening Mysticism & Protecting Our Planet," accessed October 20, 2022, https://cscommunities.org/.

13 Tim Gihring, "Lily Yeh and the Transformative Power of Art," Minneapolis Institute of Art, accessed August 20, 2023, https://new.artsmia.org/stories/lily-yeh/.

14 Joanna Macy, "Practices," Work That Reconnects Network, November 17, 2017, https://workthatreconnects.org/resources /practices/.

15 Macy, "The Story of the Elm Dance – The Work That Reconnects Communities, People & the Planet," accessed August 20, 2023, https://theworkthatreconnectssa.wordpress .com/2015/11/16/the-story-of-the-elm-dance/.

16 Trebbe Johnson, *Radical Joy for Hard Times; Finding Meaning and Making Beauty in Earth's Broken Places* (Berkeley, CA: North Atlantic Books, 2018).

17 Macy, *World as Lover, World as Self*, 4.

18 Johnson, *Radical Joy for Hard Times; Finding Meaning and Making Beauty in Earth's Broken Places*, 206.

19 Maria Popova, "Bertrand Russell on the Secret of Happiness," *The Marginalian* (blog), February 21, 2023, https://www.the marginalian.org/2023/02/21/bertrand-russell-happiness/.

SEVEN: RECLAIMING SOUL

1 Joan Chittister and Rowan Williams, *Uncommon Gratitude: Alleluia for All That Is* (Collegeville, MN: Order of Saint Benedict, 2010).

2 McAnulty, Diary of a Young Naturalist, 146–7.

3 Parker Palmer, *A Hidden Wholeness; The Journey Toward an Undivided Life* (San Francisco, CA: John Wiley, 2004), 59–60.

4 David Wagoner, *Travelling Light; Collected and New Poems* (Urbana and Chicago: University of Chicago Press, 1999), 10.

5 Gerald G. May, *The Dark Night of the Soul; A Psychiatrist Explores the Connection Between Darkness and Spiritual Growth* (New York: Harper Collins, 2004).

6 Constance Fitzgerald, OCD, "Impasse and Dark Night," 12.

7 Constance Fitzgerald, OCD, 12.

8 Constance Fitzgerald, OCD, 12.

9 Plotkin, *The Journey of Soul Initiation; A Field Guide for Visionaries, Evolutionaries, and Revolutionaries*, 2.

10 Sharon Blackie, *If Women Rose Rooted; The Journey to Authenticity and Belonging* (London: September Publishing, 2016), 132–33.

11 Plotkin, *The Journey of Soul Initiation; A Field Guide for Visionaries, Evolutionaries, and Revolutionaries*, 17.

EIGHT: COLLABORATING WITH THE LIVING WORLD

1 Carl Safina, *Becoming Wild; How Animal Cultures Raise Families, Create Beauty, and Achieve Peace* (New York: Henry Holt and Company, 2020), 104.

2 Howard Gardner's Theory of Multiple Intelligences | Center for Innovative Teaching and Learning, Northern Illinois University, accessed September 1, 2023, https://www.niu.edu /citl/resources/guides/instructional-guide/gardners-theory-of -multiple-intelligences.shtml.

3 David Abram, *The Spell of the Sensuous* (New York: Vintage Books, 1996), 48.

4 *D.J. White on Befriending a Bottlenose Dolphin*, 2023, https://www.youtube.com/watch?v=agxC7y4dy-Q.

5 Abram, *The Spell of the Sensuous*, 48.

6 Ghosh, *The Nutmeg's Curse; Parables for a Planet in Crisis*, 37–39.

7 Ghosh, 197.

8 Kathleen Dean Moore, *Earth's Wild Music; Celebrating and Defending the Songs of the Natural World* (Berkeley, CA: Counterpoint, 2021), 221–23.

9 Thomas Berry, *The Great Work: Our Way into the Future* (Crown, 2000), 55.

10 "The Four Pests Campaign: Objectives, Execution, Failure, And Consequences," WorldAtlas, April 25, 2017, https://www.worldatlas.com/articles/the-four-pests-campaign-objectives-execution-failure-and-consequences.html.

11 Debra Ronca, "How Seed Banks Work," HowStuffWorks, April 14, 2008, https://science.howstuffworks.com/environmental/green-science/seed-bank.htm.

12 Rowan White. "Reseeding the Food System; A Conversation with Rowan White," *Emergence Magazine Podcast*, November 23, 2021.

13 Suzanne Simard. *Finding the Mother Tree; Discovering the Wisdom of the Forest*. (New York: Alfred P Knopf, 2021).

14 Justin Wheeler. "Leave the Leaves." Xerces Society for Invertebrate Conservation, October 6, 2017. https://xerces.org/blog/leave-the-leaves

15 Douglas Tallamy. "Nature's Best Hope," presented to National Wildlife Federation, May 18, 2020. YouTube: https://www.youtube.com/watch?v=WY4aV5hqkxY

16 Kathy Merrifield, "The Secret Life of Soil," News story, Extension Communications (Oregon State University Extension Service, January 8, 2010), https://extension.oregonstate.edu/news/secret-life-soil.

17 "Janine Benyus—Biomimicry, an Operating Manual for Earthlings," The On Being Project, accessed April 10, 2023, https://onbeing.org/programs/janine-benyus-biomimicry-an-operating-manual-for-earthlings/.

18 *How Wolves Change Rivers*, 2014, https://www.youtube.com/watch?v=ysa5OBhXz-Q.

19 Brock Domlam and Kate Kundquist, "Beaver Believers: How to Restore Planet Water," *Bioneers* (blog), May 2, 2023, https://bioneers.org/beaver-believers-how-to-restore-planet-water/.

20 Domlam and Kundquist.

21 "Janine Benyus—"Biomimicry, an Operating Manual for Earthlings."

NINE: ON THE THRESHOLD

1 Nan Shepherd, The Living Mountain (Edinburgh: Cannongate, 2008), 8.

2 "Threshold," in *Dictionary.Com*, n.d., https://www.dictionary.com/browse/threshold.

3 David Trammel, "Predicaments and Problems | Green Wizards," accessed January 23, 2023, https://greenwizards.com/node/106.

4 Bill Plotkin, "Inscendence, Part III, SM308: Bill Plotkin Musing," Animas Valley Institute, accessed February 10, 2023, https://myemail.constantcontact.com/Inscendence—Part-III—SM308—Bill-Plotkin-Musing.html?soid=1102010840526&aid=x1iBjec5DQM.

5 Several of these practices evolved from collaboration with Shalem colleagues to lead pilgrimages. The title "pilgrimage close to home" was developed with Beth Norcross at the Center for Spirituality in Nature.

TEN: LEADERSHIP FOR EDGE TIMES

1 Bill Plotkin, "Inscendence, Part IV, SM309: Bill Plotkin Musing," Animas Valley Institute, accessed February 9, 2023, https://myemail.constantcontact.com/Inscendence—Part-IV—SM309—Bill-Plotkin-Musing.html?soid=1102010840526&aid=ajUz9ALBux8.

2 Rose Mary Dougherty, *Discernment; A Path to Spiritual Awakening* (Mahwah, NJ: Paulist Press, 2009).

3 Matthew Fox, *Creativity; Where the Divine and Human Meet* (New York: Jeremy P. Tarcher/Penguin, 2004), 77.

ELEVEN: CHOOSING STORIES FOR THE FUTURE

1 Dougald Hine, *At Work in the Ruins; Finding Our Place in the Time of Science, Climate Change, Pandemics & All Other Emergencies* (White River Junction, VT: Chelsea Green Publishing, 2023), 4, 200.

2 Emily Dickinson, "'Hope' Is the Thing with Feathers by Emily Dickinson," text/html, Poetry Foundation (Poetry Foundation, April 3, 2023), https://www.poetryfoundation.org/, https://www.poetryfoundation.org/poems/42889/hope-is-the-thing-with-feathers-314.

3 Cal Flyn, *Islands of Abandonment; Nature Rebounding in the Post-Human Landscape* (New York: Penguin Books, 2022).

4 "How Much Oxygen Comes from the Ocean?" NOAA,
  accessed August 20, 2023, https://oceanservice.noaa.gov
  /facts/ocean-oxygen.html.

5 Wall Kimmerer, *Braiding Sweetgrass; Indigenous Wisdom,
  Scientific Knowledge, and the Teachings of Plants*, 327.

6 Rebecca Solnit, "Opinion | What If Climate Change Meant Not
  Doom—but Abundance?," Washington Post, March 15, 2023,
  https://www.washingtonpost.com/opinions/2023/03/15
  /rebecca-solnit-climate-change-wealth-abundance/.

Bibliography

Abram, David. *The Spell of the Sensuous*. New York: Vintage Books, 1996.

Africa Renewal. "COP26: Landmark $500 Million Agreement Launched to Protect the DR Congo's Forest," November 10, 2021. https://www.un.org/africarenewal/magazine/ december-2021/cop26-landmark-500-million-agreement -launched-protect-dr-congo%E2%80%99s-forest.

"Atmospheric Moisture Increase | Climate Signals." Accessed August 20, 2023. https://www.climatesignals.org /climate-signals/atmospheric-moisture-increase#more.

Babu, Saurab. "Ecotones and Edges: Explaining Abrupt Changes in Ecosystems – Eco-Intelligent™." Eco-Intelligent, December 15, 2016. https://eco-intelligent. com/2016/12/15/ecotones-and-edges-explaining-abrupt -changes-in-ecosystems/.

Bass, Rick. "The Larch." In *Old Growth; The Best Writing about Trees from Orion Magazine*, 71–84. Northhampton, MA: Orion Magazine, 2021.

Bekoff, Marc. "Animal Emotions: Exploring Passionate Natures: Current Interdisciplinary Research Provides Compelling Evidence That Many Animals Experience Such Emotions as Joy, Fear, Love, Despair, and Grief— We Are Not Alone." *BioScience* 50, no. 10 (October 1, 2000): 861–70. https://doi.org/10.1641/0006–3568 (2000)050[0861:AEEPN]2.0.CO;2.

Benson, Lee. "The World's Largest and Possibly Oldest Living Organism Resides in Utah." Deseret News, August 15, 2021. https://www.deseret.com/utah/2021/8/15/22609608/worlds -largest-and-possibly-oldest-living-organism-resides-in-utah -aspens.

Beresford-Kroeger, Diana. To Speak for the Trees; My Life's Journey from Ancient Celtic Wisdom to a Healing Vision of the Forest. Toronto: Random House Canada, 2019.

Berry, Thomas. Evening Thoughts: Reflecting on Earth as a Sacred Community. Edited by Mary Evelyn Tucker. Reprint edition. San Francisco, CA: Counterpoint, 2015.

———. The Dream of the Earth. San Francisco, CA: Sierra Club Books, 1988.

———. The Great Work: Our Way into the Future. Crown, 2000.

Berry, Thomas, and Mary Evelyn Tucker. The Sacred Universe: Earth, Spirituality, and Religion in the Twenty-First Century. Columbia University Press, 2009.

———. The Sacred Universe: Earth, Spirituality, and Religion in the Twenty-First Century. New York: Columbia University Press, 2009.

Bioneers. "Intelligence in Nature: Our Family Tree of Life." Bioneers (blog), January 27, 2020. https://bioneers.org /intelligence-in-nature-zmaz2001/.

Blackie, Sharon. If Women Rose Rooted; The Journey to Authenticity and Belonging. London: September Publishing, 2016.

Blunden, Jessica. "Reporting on the State of the Climate in 2020 | NOAA Climate.gov." Accessed August 20, 2023. http://www.climate.gov/news-features/understanding-climate /reporting-state-climate-2020.

Bly, Robert, trans. Selected Poems of Rainer Maria Rilke. New York: Harper Collins, 1981.

Boehm, Sophie, and Clea Schumer. "10 Big Findings from the 2023 IPCC Report on Climate Change," March 20, 2023. https://www.wri.org/insights/2023-ipcc-ar6-synthesis-report -climate-change-findings.

Buhner, Stephen Harrod. Earth Grief; The Journey into and through Ecological Loss. Boulder, CO: Raven Press, 2022.

Burns, Chelsi. "Close-up of Tree Affected by Southern Pine Beetles—Images—USFWS National Digital Library." Accessed April 27, 2023. https://digitalmedia.fws.gov/digital/collection/natdiglib/id/27155/.

Calvin, Katherine, Dipak Dasgupta, Gerhard Krinner, Aditi Mukherji, Peter W. Thorne, Christopher Trisos, José Romero, et al. "IPCC, 2023: Climate Change 2023: Synthesis Report. Contribution of Working Groups I, II and III to the Sixth Assessment Report of the Intergovernmental Panel on Climate Change [Core Writing Team, H. Lee and J. Romero (Eds.)]. IPCC, Geneva, Switzerland." First. Intergovernmental Panel on Climate Change (IPCC), July 25, 2023. https://doi.org/10.59327/IPCC/AR6–9789291691647.

Carrington, Damian, and Damian Carrington Environment editor. "Just 3% of World's Ecosystems Remain Intact, Study Suggests." *The Guardian*, April 15, 2021, sec. Environment. https://www.theguardian.com/environment/2021/apr/15/just-3-of-worlds-ecosystems-remain-intact-study-suggests.

Center for Humans & Nature. "Entangling Humanism." Accessed January 9, 2022. https://www.humansandnature.org/entangling-humanism.

"Chincoteague National Wildlife Refuge." Accessed April 25, 2023. https://dwr.virginia.gov/vbwt/sites/chincoteague-national-wildlife-refuge/.

Chittister, Joan, and Rowan Williams. *Uncommon Gratitude: Alleluia for All That Is*. Collegeville, MN: Order of Saint Benedict, 2010.

Christie, Douglas E. *The Blue Sapphire of the Mind; Notes for a Contemplative Ecology*. New York: Oxford University Press, 2013.

Cohen, Leonard. *Selected Poems 1956–1968*. Toronto: McClelland & Stewart, 1968.

Cook, Gareth. "Why We Are Wired to Connect." Scientific American. Accessed September 14, 2022. https://www.scientificamerican.com/article/why-we-are-wired-to-connect/.

"Cosmic Calendar," February 18, 2022. https://en.wikipedia.org/wiki/Cosmic_Calendar.

"Cottonwood Tree—Kansapedia—Kansas Historical Society." Accessed January 6, 2022. https://www.kshs.org/kansapedia/cottonwood-tree/18215.

Crumley, Carole. "Shalem Institute/ Leading from within the Living Presence: The Essence of Contemplative Leadership." Shalem Institute. Accessed December 29, 2022. https://shalem.org/2016/11/15/leading-from-within-the-living-presence/

"CSC Communities – CREATION SPIRITUALITY Is about REAWAKENING MYSTICISM & PROTECTING OUR PLANET." Accessed October 20, 2022. https://cscommunities.org/.

Dean, Ann. "Shalem Institute / Mystery Taking Shape: Creativity and Contemplative Leadership." Shalem Institute. Accessed December 29, 2022. https://shalem.org/2016/11/15/mystery-taking-shape-creativity-and-contemplative-leadership.

Dean Moore, Kathleen. *Earth's Wild Music; Celebrating and Defending the Songs of the Natural World.* Berkeley, CA: Counterpoint, 2021.

Derbyshire, David. "Loneliness Is a Killer: It's as Bad for Your Health as Alcoholism, Smoking and over-Eating, Say Sceintists." *Daily Mail*, July 28, 2010. https://www.dailymail.co.uk/health/article-1298225/Loneliness-killer-Its-bad-health-alcoholism-smoking-eating-say-scientists.html.

Dickinson, Emily. "'Hope' Is the Thing with Feathers by Emily Dickinson." Text/html. Poetry Foundation. Poetry Foundation, April 3, 2023. Https://www.poetryfoundation .org/. https://www.poetryfoundation.org/poems/42889/hope-is-the-thing-with-feathers-314.

Dionne, E. J. "Opinion | The Wise Men Who Helped Me Understand Christmas." *Washington Post*, December 22, 2022. https://www.washingtonpost.com/opinions/2022/12/23/christmas-michael-gerson-mark-shields-hope/.

D.J. White on Befriending a Bottlenose Dolphin, 2023. https://www.youtube.com/watch?v=agxC7y4dy-Q.

Domlam, Brock, and Kate Kundquist. "Beaver Believers: How to Restore Planet Water." *Bioneers* (blog), May 2, 2023. https://bioneers.org/beaver-believers-how-to-restore-planet-water/.

Dougherty, Rose Mary. *Discernment; A Path to Spiritual Awakening.* Mahwah, NJ: Paulist Press, 2009.

Dyck Arboretum. "Five Oaks for the Kansas Landscape," October 29, 2014. https://dyckarboretum.org/five-oaks-for-kansas/.

"Eastern Red Cedar Berries—LocalHarvest." Accessed January 6, 2022. https://www.localharvest.org/ark/eastern-red-cedar-berries.

"Eastern Red Cedar–Know Your Enemy | NRCS Kansas." Accessed January 5, 2022. https://www.nrcs.usda.gov/wps/portal/nrcs/detail/ks/newsroom/features/?cid=nrcseprd468806.

Editorial Board. "Opinion | How to Prevent a 'Complete Doomsday' along the Colorado River." Washington Post, February 14, 2023. https://www.washingtonpost.com/opinions/2023/02/14/colorado-river-policy-solutions/.

Edwards, Tilden. "Shalem Institute / Collaboration as a Quality of Contemplative Leadership." Shalem Institute. Accessed December 29, 2022. https://shalem.org/2016/11/22 /collaboration-as-a-quality-of-contemplative-leadership.

Eliot, T.S. *Four Quartets*. New York: Houghton Mifflin, 1943.

Endangered Species Coalition. "Piping Plover." Accessed April 25, 2023. https://www.endangered.org/animals/piping-plover/.

Environment and Climate Change. "Mistaken Point Ecological Reserve and UNESCO World Heritage Site." Accessed September 1, 2022. https://www.gov.nl.ca/ecc/natural-areas /wer/r-mpe/.

Eveson, Ashley Pun. "'Eco-Grief' Emerges in New Research." The Daily Universe, April 27, 2022. https://universe.byu .edu/2022/04/26/eco-grief-emerges-in-new-research/.

Fernández Simon, Maite. "Australia Brings Animal Cruelty Charges in Mass Koala Deaths." *Washington Post*. Accessed December 25, 2021. https://www.washingtonpost.com /world/2021/12/22/koalas-animal-cruelty-australia/.

Figueiredo, Rehema. "Children More Likely to Fall out of Bed than a Tree, Daily Mail Online." Accessed September 14, 2022. https://www.dailymail.co.uk/news/article-3626687/Today-s -kids-likely-fall-bed-tree.html.

Finster, Linda Austin. "Jefferson C. Austin." *Austins of America*, February 1982.

Fitzgerald, Constance, OCD. "Impasse and Dark Night." Washington, DC: Shalem Institute for Spiritual Formation, 2016.

Flyn, Cal. *Islands of Abandonment; Nature Rebounding in the Post-Human Landscape*. New York: Penguin Books, 2022.

Forbes, Jack D. "Indigenous Americans: Spirituality and Ecos." American Academy of Arts & Sciences, Fall 2021. https://www.amacad.org/publication/ indigenous-americans-spirituality-and-ecos.

Fox, Matthew. *Creativity; Where the Divine and Human Meet*. New York: Jeremy P. Tarcher/Penguin, 2004.

———. *Original Blessing*. New York: Jeremy P. Tarcher/Putnam, 1983.

"Francis Weller and Michael Lerner—The New School at Commonweal." Accessed January 5, 2022. https://tns .commonweal.org/podcasts/weller-lerner/#.YdX_lBPMJmp.

"Garden City National Forest." In *Wikipedia*, May 10, 2021. https://en.wikipedia.org/w/index.php?title=Garden_City _National_Forest&oldid=1022369140.

ghd. "American Museum of Natural History: Cosmic Pathway." GHD Partners, September 8, 2018. https://ghdp.com/project /amonh-cosmic-pathway/.

Ghosh, Amitav. *The Nutmeg's Curse; Parables for a Planet in Crisis.* Chicago: University of Chicago Press, 2021.

Gihring, Tim. "Lily Yeh and the Transformative Power of Art." Minneapolis Institute of Art. Accessed August 20, 2023. https://new.artsmia.org/stories/lily-yeh/.

Gray, Audrey. "Nature's Say: How Voices from Hawai'i Are Reframing the Climate Conversation." *Inside Climate News*, no. February 13, 2022 (February 13, 2022). https://insideclimatenews.org/news/13022022/natures-say-how -voices-from-hawaii-are-reframing-the-climate-conversation /?utm_source=InsideClimate+News&utm_campaign=626923 aa5a-&utm_medium=email&utm_term=0_29c928ffb5 –626923aa5a-327524385Gra.

Gustin, Georgina. "The Amazon Is the Planet's Counterweight to Global Warming, a Place of Stupefying Richness Under Relentless Assault." *Inside Climate News* (blog), December 19, 2021. https://insideclimatenews.org/news/19122021 /amazon-rainforest-brazil-jair-bolsonaro-climate-change/.

Hanh, Thich Nhat. "The Insight of Interbeing |." Accessed September 1, 2023. https://www.garrisoninstitute.org/blog /insight-of-interbeing/.

Haskell, David George. *The Forest Unseen: A Year's Watch in Nature.* New York: Penguin Books, 2012.

Haupt, Lyanda Lynn. *Rooted; Life at the Crossroads of Science, Nature, and Spirit.* New York: Little, Brown Spark, 2021.

Hine, Dougald. *At Work in the Ruins; Finding Our Place in the Tim of Science, Climate Change, Pandemics, and All the Other Emergencies.* White River Junction, VT: Chelsea Green Publishing, 2023.

Horn, Gavin Van, Robin Wall Kimmerer, and John Hausdoerffer, eds. *Kinship; Belonging in a World of Relations.* Vol. 01, Planet. 05 vols. Libertyville, IL: Center for Humans and Nature PRess, 2021.

"How Many Species Are We Losing?" Accessed August 20, 2023. https://wwf.panda.org/discover/our_focus/biodiversity /biodiversity.

How Wolves Change Rivers, 2014. https://www.youtube.com /watch?v=ysa5OBhXz-Q.

hsotr. "A Forest in Western Kansas." *Homestead on the Range* (blog), September 30, 2014. https://homesteadontherange .com/2014/09/30/a-forest-in-western-kansas/.

https://www.apa.org. "Addressing Climate Change Concerns in Practice." Accessed July 29, 2022. https://www.apa.org /monitor/2021/03/ce-climate-change.

https://www.apa.org. "Majority of US Adults Believe Climate Change Is Most Important Issue Today." Accessed July 29, 2022. https://www.apa.org/news/press/releases/2020/02 /climate-change.

Ianzito, Christina. "Former Surgeon General Vivek Murthy on Loneliness." AARP. Accessed September 14, 2022. https://www.aarp.org/health/healthy-living/info-2020/vivek -murthy-loneliness.html.

Ignatian Solidarity Network. "Canticle of Brother Sun and Sister Moon of St. Francis of Assisi," June 4, 2015. https://ignatiansolidarity.net/blog/2015/06/04/canticle-of -brother-sun-and-sister-moon-of-st-francis-of-assisi/.

"Infographics—Screen Time vs. Lean Time | DNPAO | CDC," January 23, 2019. https://www.cdc.gov/nccdphp/dnpao /multimedia/infographics/getmoving.html.

"It's Official: July Was Earth's Hottest Month on Record," August 13, 2021. https://www.noaa.gov/news/its-official-july -2021-was-earths-hottest-month-on-record.

Joanna Macy and Chris Johnstone. *Active Hope; How to Face the Mess We're in without Going Crazy*. Novato, CA: New World Library, 2012.

Johnsgard, Paul. *Sandhill and Whooping Cranes; Ancient Voices over America's Wetlands*. Lincoln, NE: University of Nebraska Press, 2011.

Johnson, Trebbe. *Radical Joy for Hard Times; Finding Meaning and Making Beauty in Earth's Broken Places*. Berkeley, CA: North Atlantic Books, 2018.

Jones, Benji. "IPCC: Climate Change Is Driving a Mass

Extinction—Vox." Accessed February 20, 2023.
https://www.vox.com/down-to-earth/2022/3/1/22954531
/climate-change-ipcc-wildlife-extinction.

Jones, Lucy. "Creatures That Don't Conform – Lucy Jones."
Emergence Magazine, February 2, 2023. https:/
/emergencemagazine.org/essay/creatures-that-dont-conform/.

Joseph, Bob. "What Is the Seventh Generation Principle?"
Accessed April 15, 2022. https://www.ictinc.ca/blog
/seventh-generation-principle.

Kaplan, Sarah, and Andrew Ba Tran. "Nearly 1 in 3 Americans
Experienced a Weather Disaster This Summer." Washington
Post, September 4, 2021. https://www.washingtonpost.com
/climate-environment/2021/09/04/climate-disaster
-hurricane-ida/.

Keltner, Dacher. *Awe: The New Science of Everyday Wonder
and How It Can Transform Your Life.* New York: Penguin
Books, 2023.

Keppel, Gunnar, Kimberly P. Van Niel, Grant W. Wardell-Johnson,
Colin J. Yates, Margaret Byrne, Ladislav Mucina,
Antonius G. T. Schut, Stephen D. Hopper, and Steven E.
Franklin. "Refugia: Identifying and Understanding Safe
Havens for Biodiversity under Climate Change." *Global
Ecology and Biogeography* 21, no. 4 (2012): 393–404.
https://doi.org/10.1111/j.1466–8238.2011.00686.x.

KFF. "Daily Media Use Among Children and Teens Up
Dramatically from Five Years Ago," January 20, 2010.
https://www.kff.org/racial-equity-and-health-policy
/press-release/daily-media-use-among-children-and-teens-up
-dramatically-from-five-years-ago/.

King, Martin Luther. "Christmas Sermon on Peace."
Presented at the Ebenezer Baptist ChurchChris, Atlanta, GA,
December 24, 1964. https://speakola.com/ideas/martin
-luther-king-jr-interconnected-world-massey-5–1967.

Klinkenborg, Verlyn. "The Forest's Eye View." *The New York
Review of Books* LXIX, no. 12 (July 21, 2022): 33–35.

Krawec, Patty. *Becoming Kin: An Indigenous Call to Unforgetting
the Past and Reimagining Our Future.* Minneapolis, MN:
Broadleaf Books, 2022.

Leopold, Aldo. *A Sand County Almanac.* New York: Random House, 1949.

Levine-Drizin, Gabe, and Adam Johnson. "TV News Did More Stories on Queen Elizabeth II in the Past 2 Weeks Than on Climate Change in the Past 2 Years." Substack newsletter. *The Column* (blog), September 22, 2022. https://thecolumn .substack.com/p/tv-news-did-more-stories-on-queen.

Levitt, Zach, and Bonnie Berkowitz. "Cold, Heat, Fires, Hurricanes and Tornadoes: The Year in Weather Disasters." Washington Post. Accessed August 20, 2023. https://www.washingtonpost .com/nation/interactive/2021/weather-disasters-2021/.

Lindsay, Rebecca. "Climate Change: Atmospheric Carbon Dioxide | NOAA Climate.gov." Accessed August 20, 2023. http://www.climate.gov/news-features/understanding-climate /climate-change-atmospheric-carbon-dioxide.

Lohman, Meg. *The Arbornaut; A Life Discovering the Eighth Continent in the Trees Above Us.* New York: Farrar, Straus, and Giroux, 2021.

"Loneliness Is a Killer: It's as Bad for Your Health as Alcoholism, Smoking and over-Eating, Say Scientists | Daily Mail Online." Accessed April 1, 2022. https://www.dailymail.co.uk/health /article-1298225/Loneliness-killer-Its-bad-health-alcoholism -smoking-eating-say-scientists.html.

Look Inside a Rattlesnake's Rattle | Deep Look, 2019. https://www.youtube.com/watch?v=ZO4IAZycUik.

MacGillis, Miriam, and Rhonda Fabian. "An Interview with Sister Miriam Therese MacGillis at Genesis Farm." *Kosmos Journal* (blog), Summer 2017. https://www.kosmosjournal.org/article /an-interview-with-sister-miriam-therese-macgillis-at-genesis-farm/.

Maclean, Ruth, and Dionne Searcey. "Congo to Auction Land to Oil Companies: 'Our Priority Is Not to Save the Planet.'" *The New York Times*, July 24, 2022, sec. World. https://www.nytimes .com/2022/07/24/world/africa/congo-oil-gas-auction.html.

Macy, Joanna. "Inalienable: Belonging to the Earth Community." Bioneers. Accessed March 12, 2022. https://bioneers.org /inalienable-belonging-to-the-earth-community-joanna-macy/.

———. "Joanna Macy on Healing Begins with Gratitude." *The Mountain Hermitage* (blog), December 7, 2018. https://mountainhermitage .org/2018/12/07/joanna-macy-healing-begins-gratitude/.

———. "Practices." Work That Reconnects Network, November 17, 2017. https://workthatreconnects.org/resources/practices/.

————. "The Story of the Elm Dance – The Work That Reconnects Communities, People & the Planet." Accessed August 20, 2023. https://theworkthatreconnectssa.wordpress.com/2015/11/16/the-story-of-the-elm-dance/.

————. "Work That Reconnects; Personal Guidelines," n.d. https://workthatreconnects.org/spiral/the-great-turning/personal-guidelines/.

————. *World as Lover, World as Self.* Berkeley, CA: Parallax Press, 1991.

Makower, Joel. "Climate Change and the New Language of Weather | Greenbiz." Accessed August 20, 2023. https://www.greenbiz.com/article/climate-change-and-new-language-weather.

"Man Spends Four Days Making a Visual Representation Of History In Which One Domino Equals One Million Years—Digg." Accessed January 26, 2022. https://digg.com/video/history-universe-dominoes.

Mark, Joshua J. "Hildegard of Bingen." In *World History Encyclopedia*, May 30, 2019. https://www.worldhistory.org/Hildegard_of_Bingen/.

May, Gerald G. *The Dark Night of the Soul; A Psychiatrist Explores the Connection Between Darkness and Spiritual Growth.* New York: Harper Collins, 2004.

————. *The Wisdom of Wilderness; Experiencing the Healing Power of Nature.* San Francisco, CA: Harper San Francisco, 2006.

McAnulty, Dara. *Diary of a Young Naturalist.* Minneapolis, MN: Milkweed Edition, 2022.

McNerthney, Casey. "Heat Wave Broils Western Washington, Shattering Seattle and Regional." Accessed August 20, 2023. https://www.historylink.org/File/21266.

Meade, Michael. "Awakening the Genius in Everyone: When the Calling Keeps Calling | Michael Meade." *Bioneers* (blog), October 25, 2017. https://bioneers.org/awakening-the-genius-in-everyone-when-the-calling-keeps-calling-michael-meade/.

Meade, Michael. *Why the World Doesn't End; Tales of Renewal in Times of Loss.* Seattle, WA: GreenFire Press, 2012.

Merrifield, Kathy. "The Secret Life of Soil." News story. Extension Communications. Oregon State University Extension Service, January 8, 2010. https://extension.oregonstate.edu/news/secret-life-soil.

Merton, Thomas. *Conjectures of a Guilty Bystander*. New York: Doubleday, 1966.

———. *The Hidden Ground of Love; The Letters of Thomas Merton*. New York: Farrar, Straus, and Giroux, 2011.

Mora, Gia. "Edge Effects: Habitat Biodiversity and Human Interference." Treehugger. Accessed February 28, 2023. https://www.treehugger.com/what-are-edge-effects-6361690.

Morris, Steven. "Back to Nature: 'Secret Garden' Outings Used to Aid Coronavirus Recovery." *The Guardian*, May 5, 2020, sec. World news. https://www.theguardian.com/world/2020/may/05/back-to-nature-secret-garden-outings-used-to-aid-coronavirus-recovery.

Narby, Jeremy. *Nature's Intelligence: Coming Down from the Pedestal | Jeremy Narby and J.P. Harpignies*. Accessed December 24, 2022. https://soundcloud.com/bioneers/natures-intelligence-coming-down-from-the-pedestal-jeremy-narby-and-jp-harpignies.

Newell, John Philip. *Sacred Earth Sacred Soul; Celtic Wisdom for Reawakening to What Our Souls Know and Healing the World*. New York: HarperOne, 2021.

Niznik Behavioral Health. "Self-Medicating in America." Accessed September 19, 2022. https://www.niznikhealth.com/research-articles/self-medicating-in-america/.

NOAA. "How Much Oxygen Comes from the Ocean?" Accessed August 20, 2023. https://oceanservice.noaa.gov/facts/ocean-oxygen.html.

Northern Illinois University. "Howard Gardner's Theory of Multiple Intelligences | Center for Innovative Teaching and Learning." Accessed September 1, 2023. https://www.niu.edu/citl/resources/guides/instructional-guide/gardners-theory-of-multiple-intelligences.shtml.

"Noxious Weed | Russell County, KS." Accessed August 20, 2023. https://russellcountykansas.com/201/Noxious-Weed.

Old Growth; The Best Writing about Trees from Orion Magazine. Northhampton, MA: Orion Magazine, 2021.

O'Shea, Claire. "NASA Clocks July 2023 as Hottest Month on Record Ever Since 1880." Text. NASA, August 14, 2023. http://www.nasa.gov/press-release/nasa-clocks-july-2023-as-hottest-month-on-record-ever-since-1880.

Otto Scharmer, and Katrin Kaufer. *Leading from the Emerging Future; From Ego-System to Eco-System Economies*. Oakland, CA: Berrett-Koehler Publishers Inc, 2013.

Palmer, Parker. *A Hidden Wholeness; The Journey Toward an Undivided Life*. San Francisco, CA: John Wiley, 2004.

Parr, Jackson. "Journey of a Lifetime: The Great Migration of the Monarch Butterfly." Door County Pulse, June 30, 2016. https://doorcountypulse.com/journey-lifetime-great -migration-monarch-butterfly/.

Paulson, Steve. "Living in Mystery" In Interview with Marcelo Gleiser." In *Kinship; Belonging in a World of Relationships*, 1:74–83. Planet. Libertyville, IL: Center for Humans and Nature Press, 2021.

Plastic Oceans International. "Plastic Oceans: The Facts." Accessed August 14, 2022. https://plasticoceans.org/the-facts/.

Plotkin, Bill. "Inscendence, Part III, SM308: Bill Plotkin Musing." Animas Valley Institute. Accessed February 10, 2023. https://myemail.constantcontact.com/Inscendence—Part-III —SM308—Bill-Plotkin-Musing.html?soid=1102010840526 &aid=x1iBjec5DQM.

———. "Inscendence, Part IV, SM309: Bill Plotkin Musing." Animas Valley Institute. Accessed February 9, 2023. https://myemail .constantcontact.com/Inscendence—Part-IV—SM309—Bill -Plotkin-Musing.html?soid=1102010840526&aid=ajUz9ALBux8.

———. *The Journey of Soul Initiation; A Field Guide for Visionaries, Evolutionaries, and Revolutionaries*. Novato, CA: New World Library, 2021.

Popova, Maria. "Barry Lopez on the Cure for Our Existential Loneliness and the Three Tenets of a Full Life." *The Marginalian* (blog), September 18, 2022. https://www .themarginalian.org/2022/09/18/barry-lopez-place-loneliness/.

———. "Bertrand Russell on the Secret of Happiness." *The Marginalian* (blog), February 21, 2023. https://www. themarginalian.org/2023/02/21/bertrand-russell-happiness/.

———. "Gmail—The Antidote to the Time-Anxiety That Savages Our Lives; the Neuroscience of How the Body Moves the Mind and How Our Feelings Shape Our Consciousness." Accessed December 26, 2021. https://mail.google.com /mail/u/0/?ui=2&ik=ddd4cc2938&view=lg&permmsgid =msg-f:1720206183767809459.

Portland Japanese Garden. "Shinrin-Yoku: The Simple and Intuitive Form of Preventative Care," August 15, 2022. https://japanesegarden.org/2022/08/15/shinrin-yoku/.

Quinn, James A. "An Abstract of The Journal of John Woolman." Accessed January 13, 2022. https://www.friendsjournal.org /legacy/abington/gwynedd/John_Woolman.html.

Rampy, Leah. "Coming to Our Senses; Embracing Awe and Wonder" in *Soul Food; Nourishing Essays on Contemplative Living and Leadership,* edited by Westina Matthews, Margaret Benefiel, and Jackson Droney, 119–130. New York: Church Publishing, 2023.

———. "Shalem Institute / Contemplative Leadership: Compassion, Power & Hope." Shalem Institute. Accessed December 29, 2022. https://shalem.org/2013/02/22 /contemplative-leadership-compassion-power-hope.

Rawlence, Ben. *The Treeline; The Last Forest and the Future of Life on Earth.* New York: St. Martin's Press, 2022.

Reid, John W. and Lovejoy, Thomas E. *Ever Green; Saving Big Forests to Save the Planet.* New York: W.W. Norton, 2022.

Reo, Devika. "The Extreme Weather Events of 2023." The Week. Accessed August 31, 2023. https://theweek.com/in-depth /1021278/2023-extreme-weather.

Rilke, Rainer Maria. *Rilke's Book of Hours: Love Poems to God.* New York: Riverhead Books, 2005.

Ripley, Amanda. "Opinion | This Element Is Critical to Human Flourishing—yet Missing from the News." Washington Post, March 30, 2023. https://www.washingtonpost.com/opinions/2023/03/30 /amanda-ripley-hope-news/.

Ronca, Debra. "How Seed Banks Work." HowStuffWorks, April 14, 2008. https://science.howstuffworks.com /environmental/green-science/seed-bank.htm.

Root, Tik. "Interested in Protecting Old-Growth Forests? Here Are Some Steps You Can Take." *Washington Post,* January 7, 2022. https://www.washingtonpost.com/climate-environment/2022 /01/07/save-trees-old-growth-forest-timber/.

RRC. "Refugia Research Coalition." Accessed April 25, 2023. https://www.climaterefugia.org.

Safina, Carl. *Becoming Wild; How Animal Cultures Raise Families, Create Beauty, and Achieve Peace*. New York: Henry Holt and Company, 2020.

Salmon, Enrique. "Kincentric Ecology: Indigenous Perceptions of the Human-Nature Relationship." *Ecological Applications* 10, no. 5 (October 2000): 1327. https://doi.org/10.2307/2641288.

Samenow, Jason. "Lightning Gone Wild during D.C.'s Derecho." *Washington Post* (blog), June 29, 2023. https://www.washingtonpost.com/blogs/capital-weather-gang/post/lightning-gone-wild-during-dcs-derecho/2012/07/02/gJQACeuqIW_blog.html.

"Science Explains 12 Benefits of Keeping a Gratitude Journal." Accessed August 30, 2022. https://www.powerofpositivity.com/science-explains-12-benefits-gratitude-journal/.

Searing, Linda. "Loneliness Can Increase Risk of Heart Disease by 27 Percent for Older Women." *Washington Post*. Accessed September 14, 2022. https://www.washingtonpost.com/health/2022/02/20/loneliness-heart-disease-older-women/.

"Secretary-General Calls Latest IPCC Climate Report 'Code Red for Humanity', Stressing 'Irrefutable' Evidence of Human Influence | UN Press." Accessed August 20, 2023. https://press.un.org/en/2021/sgsm20847.doc.htm.

Shalem Institute. "Shalem Institute / Contemplative Leadership." Accessed December 29, 2022. https://shalem.org/2013/02/22/contemplative-leadership.

Sheldrake, Merlin. *Entangled Life; How Fungi Make Our Worlds, Change Our Minds & Shape Our Futures*. New York: Random House, 2020.

Shepherd, Nan. *The Living Mountain*. Edinburgh: Cannongate, 2008.

Simard, Suzanne. *Finding the Mother Tree; Discovering the Wisdom of the Forest*. New York: Alfred P. Knopf, 2021.

Simmons, Joe, SJ. "'Where Is the Love?' Or 'Prayer: A Long Loving Look at the Real'—The Jesuit Post," January 29, 2012. https://thejesuitpost.org/2012/01/where-is-the-love-or-prayer-a-long-loving-look-at-the-real/.

Sly, Eleanor. "Nearly One-Third of Tree Species at Risk of Extinction," August 31, 2021.

Solnit, Rebecca. "Opinion | What If Climate Change Meant Not Doom—but Abundance?" Washington Post, March 15, 2023. https://www.washingtonpost.com/opinions/2023/03/15/rebecca-solnit-climate-change-wealth-abundance/.

SOS: Save Our Soil. "SOS: Save Our Soil." Accessed May 4, 2023. https://www.saveoursoilwv.com/.

St. George, Donna. "Md. Officials: Letting 'Free Range' Kids Walk or Play Alone Is Not Neglect—The Washington Post." Accessed September 19, 2022. https://www.washingtonpost.com/local/education/state-seeks-to-clarify-views-about-young-children-walking-alone/2015/06/11/423ce72c-0b99-11e5-95fd-d580f1c5d44e_story.html.

Statista. "Time Spent with Media in the U.S. 2022." Accessed May 17, 2023. https://www.statista.com/statistics/278544/time-spent-with-media-in-the-us/.

Steindl-Rast, Brother David. Words of Common Sense for Mind, Body and Soul. West Conshohocken, PA: Templeton Press, 2002.

Stillman, Dan. "The Great Salt Lake Seemed like It Was Dying. But There's Been a 'Miraculous' Shift." Washington Post, April 9, 2023. https://www.washingtonpost.com/weather/2023/04/09/great-salt-lake-snowpack-water-level/.

Sundberg, Maureen. "A Chickadee's Guide to Gardening: How to Create Habitat for Birds in Urban Settings." Ecological Landscape Alliance (blog), October 15, 2019. https://www.ecolandscaping.org/10/landscaping-for-wildlife/wildlife-habitats/a-chickadees-guide-to-gardening-how-to-create-habitat-for-birds-in-urban-settings/.

TalkDeath. "Ecological Grief: Mourning the Loss of Our Planet," August 3, 2020. https://www.talkdeath.com/ecological-grief-mourning-loss-our-planet/.

Tallamy, Douglas W. Nature's Best Hope; A New Approach to Conservation That Starts in Your Yard. Portland, OR: Timber Press, Inc., 2019.

Taylor, Bron. "Kinship through the Senses, Arts, and Sciences." In Kinship; Belonging in a World of Relations, 1:30–47. Libertyville, IL: Center for Humans and Nature Press, 2021.

Teilhard de Chardin, Pierre. *The Divine Milieu.* New York: Harper Torch Books, 1960.

The Museum of the Cherokee Indian. "Trail of Tears." Accessed September 20, 2022. https://mci.org/archives/era/trail-of-tears.

The On Being Project. "Suzanne Simard—Forests Are Wired For Wisdom." Accessed January 2, 2022. https://onbeing.org/programs/suzanne-simard-forests-are-wired-for-wisdom/.

"The Pros and Cons of the Eastern Redcedar | Piedmont Master Gardeners." Accessed January 6, 2022. https://piedmontmastergardeners.org/article/the-pros-and-cons-of-the-eastern-redcedar/.

"Threshold." In *Dictionary.Com*, n.d. https://www.dictionary.com/browse/threshold.

Thrive. "Forest Bathing: What It Is and Why You Should Try It." Accessed September 1, 2022. https://thrive.kaiserpermanente.org/thrive-together/live-well/forest-bathing-try.

Tonino, Leath. "The Sun Magazine | The Egret Lifting From The River; David Hinton on the Wisdom of Ancient Chinese Poets | Issue 469." The Sun Magazine, January 2015. https://www.thesunmagazine.org/issues/469/the-egret-lifting-from-the-river.

Trahant, Mark. "How Colonization of the Americas Killed 90 Percent of Their Indigenous People—and Changed the Climate." *YES! Magazine* (blog). Accessed September 20, 2022. https://www.yesmagazine.org/opinion/2019/02/13/how-colonization-of-the-americas-killed-90-percent-of-their-indigenous-people-and-changed-the-climate.

Trammel, David. "Predicaments and Problems | Green Wizards." Accessed January 23, 2023. https://greenwizards.com/node/106.

"UCSF Sustainability." Accessed July 29, 2022. https://sustainability.ucsf.edu/1.830.

United States Now. "How Has the Average Size of American Homes Changed over Time?" Accessed September 19, 2022. http://www.unitedstatesnow.org/how-has-the-average-size-of-american-homes-changed-over-time.htm.

unknown. "The Importance of Snakes." Environment | Department of Environment and Science, Queensland. jurisdiction=Queensland; sector=government; corporateName=Department of

Environment and Science, October 4, 2011. https://environment
.des.qld.gov.au/wildlife/animals/living-with/snakes/importance.

"US Media Consumption (2018–2024) [Updated Aug 2022] |
Oberlo." Accessed September 19, 2022. https://www.oberlo
.com/statistics/us-media-consumption.

"USDA ERS—Irrigation & Water Use." Accessed April 4, 2023.
https://www.ers.usda.gov/topics/farm-practices-management
/irrigation-water-use/.

Vescio, Michael. "The Historic Derecho of June 29, 2012."
Department of Commerce. Accessed August 10, 2023. https://www
.weather.gov/media/publications/assessments/derecho12.pdf.

Wagoner, David. *Travelling Light; Collected and New Poems.*
Urbana and Chicago: University of Chicago Press, 1999.

Wall Kimmerer, Robin. *Braiding Sweetgrass; Indigenous Wisdom,
Scientific Knowledge, and the Teachings of Plants.* Minneapolis,
MN: Milkweed Editions, 2013.

———. "How the Myth of Human Exceptionalism Cut Us Off
From Nature." *Literary Hub* (blog), September 21, 2022.
https://lithub.com/robin-wall-kimmerer-humans-nature/.

———. "The Serviceberry: An Economy of Abundance – Robin
Wall Kimmerer." Emergence Magazine, October 26, 2022.
https://emergencemagazine.org/essay/the-serviceberry/.

Ward, Liz. "Shalem Institute / Opening to God: Receiving Nurture
for Contemplative Leadership." Shalem Institute. Accessed
December 29, 2022. https://shalem.org/2016/11/22/opening
-to-god-receiving-nurture-for-contemplative-leadership.

Weller, Francis, and Michael Lerner. "The Long Dark: Tending
to the Soul in Unknown Territory." The New School at
Commonweal, November 12, 2021. https://tns.commonweal
.org/podcasts/weller-lerner/.

"West Virginia Northern Flying Squirrel." Accessed May 8, 2022.
https://www.biologicaldiversity.org/species/mammals/West
_Virginia_northern_flying_squirrel/index.html.

"When a Thin Place Discovers Us | The Journal of Wild Culture."
Accessed January 9, 2022. https://www.wildculture.com/article
/when-thin-place-discovers-us/1946.

"Why We Need a Healthy Planet." Accessed August 20, 2023.
https://livingplanet.panda.org/en-US/impact.

"Witless Bay Ecological Reserve—Environment and Climate Change," October 23, 2020. https://www.gov.nl.ca/ecc /natural-areas/wer/r-wbe/.

Wohlleben. *The Hidden Language of Trees; What They Feel, How They Communicate.* Translated by Jane Billinghurst. Berkeley, CA: Greystone Books, 2015.

WorldAtlas. "The Four Pests Campaign: Objectives, Execution, Failure, And Consequences," April 25, 2017. https://www.worldatlas.com/articles/the-four-pests-campaign -objectives-execution-failure-and-consequences.html.

"WWF—Building a Future in Which Humans Live in Harmony with Nature." Accessed August 20, 2023. https://wwf.panda.org/.

www.dictionary.com. "Definition of Nature | Dictionary.Com." Accessed December 23, 2022. https://www.dictionary.com /browse/nature.

www.fao.org. "The State of the World's Forests 2020." Accessed August 31, 2023. https://doi.org/10.4060/CA8642EN.

Yale Program on Climate Change Communication. "Global Warming's Six Americas, September 2021." Accessed January 14, 2022. https://climatecommunication.yale.edu/publications /global-warmings-six-americas-september-2021/.

About the Author

Leah Rampy is a writer, retreat leader, and educator who weaves ecology, spirituality, personal stories, and practices to help others deepen their relationship to the natural world. After offering numerous presentations on climate change, she began a decades-long journey to understand what lies beneath our unwillingness to change our interactions with the natural world. Her growing commitment to reconnecting Earth and soul has been informed by leading over a dozen pilgrimages and many more retreats, extensive reading and research, her contemplative practice, and the wisdom of the living world.

Rampy has taught in public schools and universities, held leadership roles in Fortune 100 companies, offered executive coaching and leadership consulting through a company she founded, and led a nonprofit organization. She is the founder and leader of *Church of the Wild Two Rivers* that meets monthly outdoors to deepen spirituality in kinship with nature. Rampy holds a Ph.D. in Curriculum from Indiana University. She lives with her husband in a cohousing community in Shepherdstown, WV. The Rampys have two adult children.

About
Bold Story Press

Bold Story Press is a curated, woman-owned hybrid publishing company with a mission of publishing well-written stories by women. If your book is chosen for publication, our team of expert editors and designers will work with you to publish a professionally edited and designed book. Every woman has a story to tell. If you have written yours and want to explore publishing with Bold Story Press, contact us at https://boldstorypress.com.

**BOLD
STORY
PRESS**

The Bold Story Press logo, designed by Grace Arsenault, was inspired by the nom de plume, or pen name, a sad necessity at one time for female authors who wanted to publish. The woman's face hidden in the quill is the profile of Virginia Woolf, who, in addition to being an early feminist writer, founded and ran her own publishing company, Hogarth Press.

54743619R00130